Thirty-Three Years

before

THE MAST

THIRTY-THREE YEARS
before
THE MAST

*The Observations and Experiences
of an Unrepentant Sensei*

Michael Angelo, Ph.D.

Rutledge Books, Inc.

Danbury, CT

ALL RIGHTS RESERVED
Rutledge Books, Inc.
107 Mill Plain Road, Danbury, CT 06811
1-800-278-8533
www.rutledgebooks.com

Manufactured in the United States of America

Cataloging in Publication Data
Angelo, Michael

   Thirty-Three Years Before the Mast

   ISBN: 1-58244-146-4

   1. Memoir -- Teacher. 2. Public Education -- Schools --
America. 3. Current Crisis -- Education.

Library of Congress Card Number: 2001086397

Contents

$\mathscr{I}$ntroduction

At no one's particular behest and with the unrelenting encouragement of my wife I have put together a chronicle which is a compilation of personal experiences, opinions, and observations regarding education in the United States. As the title of this book states, thirty-three years of my life have been spent laboring in the gardens of academe. And as it is with most of my professional breed it is my belief that I have something to say! What's more, I believe that some lost soul(s) may actually be interested in what I have to say.

As a former upstate New York Social Studies teacher in a suburban high school environment, I am keenly aware of my limitations. These include minimal urban classroom contact, minimal minority student contact, and minimal private school familiarity. This aside, it is my firm conviction that participation with and exposure to the American student during four distinct decades from the 1960s through the 1990s, qualifies me at least as quasi-knowledgeable in the "education game."

My personal acquaintance with the Asian "connection" gives me the opportunity to make unscientific but I believe valid comparisons to our own education system. The author's admiration for the Japanese culture and its educational system, warts and all, will persistently make itself manifest. My apologies to those who still harbor negative feelings toward a former enemy and fierce competitor.

The labor-management "card" will turn up frequently due to the author's personal involvement in the public sector from its inception. As a negotiator, committee representative, building representative, and, finally, grievance chair for twenty years there was little in the way of labor-management relations that I missed out on. It was in this role that the total educational spectrum was revealed to me. Boards of Education, superintendents, administrators, teachers, monitors, janitors, bus drivers, and whoever I have failed to recall became a real part of my world which previously had suffered from "tunnel-vision" of a professional sort.

The text will reflect not only upon the writer's experiences and observations in the public school arena but will include recommendations/proposals that the author considers, in all humility, to offer an effective alternative and/or modification of existing pedagogical practices and institutional organizational goals.

It is the earnest hope of the author that in some meaningful, even if minute manner, the ensuing chapters will contribute towards a clearer understanding of the possibilities that still lie ahead for the world's greatest egalitarian experiment in education and living.

Chapter One

The Early Years

1

Did I Make the Right Decision?

Invariably whenever I am with a group of friends or close associates and the conversation turns toward educational issues, more often than not the question will be posed to me: "If you had it to do over again, would you go into teaching?" For me, the reply is an instantaneous and unequivocal, "YES!" I realize unfortunately that for a growing number of my fellow colleagues throughout the nation the response is neither instantaneous nor necessarily positive. During the course of this book the reasons for both responses will be explored.

When I entered the teaching profession at the outset of the sixties I was totally unaware of the status of teaching or teachers in terms of society's assessment. As I look back on my decision to become a teacher I cannot recall ever wanting to be anything else, except to play in Yankee Stadium. It seemed so natural, unlike today when we talk of teachers being role models because it makes us comfortable with our illusions. Teachers, four decades ago actually were role models to parents and kids alike. I can still recall practically all of my elementary teachers' names as well as my junior high and senior high school teachers. That was over forty years ago. I recall the good ones and the bad ones. As I reminisce on the qualities of both, I am struck by a thread of commonality which pervaded almost each one, and that was the perception on my part that they really cared for me, despite the fact that I was one of the perennial candidates for the faculty's Preparation H Award. As William Faulkner observed in the preface to one of his novels that it had been his experience to have had only a few great teachers in his youth, but they had, "...made all the difference..." So it was with me.

The source of my inspiration came from two divergent disciplines, athletics and English. Not unlike many boys who had the good fortune to participate for one reason or another in interscholastic competition, they were fortunate indeed if they had a mentor/guide similar to my physical education teacher in high school. We called him 'Prof'. No one really knew or cared why, but we all said it to his face as well as when he wasn't in our presence with a feeling of respect and warmth. Over the years I have often contemplated, in retrospect, what qualities this man possessed that made me admire him and influence my decision to become a teacher and a coach. I believe, although I could not articulate it at the time, that it was his ability to make us feel that he cared. Strangely enough, it was not on the competitive playing field that his sense of concern displayed itself in its most effective form, but in our physical education classes. Despite the fact that our gym class had many of the star athletes who played on Prof's teams, he treated us as individuals and as equals.

Whether you were an athlete or not; slow, fat, weak, or shy you knew that Prof was looking out for you. One talent that he possessed, and which I subconsciously emulated in my own classroom years later, was his uncanny knack of knowing when to be an informal and supportive friend and when it was equally necessary to be a stern, but fair, disciplinarian. This, as I recognized later as a classroom teacher, was an effective tool for drawing-in students but not too close. It is a method, although I suspect that for Prof it was just him being himself, which can effectively maintain discipline within a personal context. I firmly believe that the gap between student and teacher must always be maintained. There must never be a blurring of the line of demarcation. The student and the teacher must develop a feeling of mutual respect within the context of the subject matter or discipline under study; both teacher and student become fused in their mutual quest for knowledge and truth. Their roles/identities may differ but their quest for the Holy Grail is identical.

When I entered college as an undergraduate in the fall of 1956, I naturally matriculated into the School of Physical Education and Health. I wanted to be a coach and play football. I believed that I was eminently qualified to do both. I loved telling people what and how to do things and my physical bulk and mental attitude was such that the mere thought of running into and over other humans brought a feeling of sheer ecstasy to me.

Our college football team, as I learned upon my arrival, had fallen upon hard times for over a decade. It was a standing joke on campus that our rivals organized their schedules so that we would make their homecoming weekend a success. And then in 1958, a new football coach and rather remarkable man arrived on campus. When we arrived for preseason practice we were somewhat apprehensive as to what kind of coach he would be. What were his expectations of us as individuals? Would some of us be shifted to other positions? What kind of an offense, defense did he run? How long would it take him to know us? It didn't take long. He had reviewed all of our previous year's films by position and, scary as it seemed both then and now, he really knew who we were—our names, our strengths, weaknesses and most of all our potential. He took a 2-6 loser from the previous year with almost identical returning personnel and turned us into a 7-1 team which would lead the nation in total defense in 1958.

The metamorphosis from losers to winners was not limited to the playing field. If that had been the case, I would not be taking the time to recount a mere winning season of football. That year marked Year One in many of our young lives. For our small campus, that fall of 1958 was a turning point in peoples' attitudes not only towards a football team but towards the college itself. How had it occurred? Later in my professional life as a social science teacher, whenever the Great Man Theory of history was debated, my thoughts without exception always drifted towards my college football coach. He had imbued within us the making of a community. He had give us a raison d'être. It was not the mere winning of an athletic contest, although it is obvious that such was required, but it was the idea that we were involved in a Herculean task that would demand of each of us an examination of and subsequent summoning of our innermost spiritual and physical stamina in our collective quest as a TEAM. For the first time in our lives all of us who had played on other teams became a viable, contributing, and vital member of a TEAM. Everybody played. Every player had a niche. And most of all, that man made each of us—from our 125 lb. third-string quarterback to our premier All-American center—believe that alone we were nothing, but together we were invincible.

Collectively and individually we feared losing, not only because of its negative affect on the season but because we had failed him and by doing so had failed ourselves. HE never shouted. He never ranted or raved. His pep talks were not of the Rockne variety; they were calm and coherent, addressing technical problems, and proposing measured and rational solutions. He talked to each of us separately. He made us believe in ourselves and in the nobility of our cause. He knew that years later when we would fulfill the roles of husband, father, grandparent, and teacher that the process of winning would serve as our principal guide and allow us to instill in others that same commitment which had become his legacy to us: the desire and need to excel as individuals and to be accountable to and for each other. Cain had been answered.

Whenever there is a gathering of two or more of his players from any of the teams he coached, the conversation inevitably comes to those remembrances of a man who in so many ways, both overtly and subtly, influenced the molding and direction of our personal and professional lives. He left us prematurely in 1975, dying of a massive heart failure at the age of 51. For those of us who were touched by his presence and had the opportunity to experience his light he will always be with us.

They called her Ma. She was a statuesque woman standing close to six feet tall, or so it seemed. By the time I reached high school in my hometown as a sophomore—three-year high schools were still in vogue—she was already a legend. Upon receiving my assignment schedule I found that the next three years of homeroom would be spent with her. Although at the time I would not know it, my year of junior English would also be spent in her company. Little did I know at the time that this most feared of God's feminine creations would exert upon me the greatest influence on how I would conduct myself in the future as a teacher.

When you entered her classroom it was like entering a religious sanctuary. She had the knack of making attendance taking feel like being placed under a bright light alone with the Grand Inquisitor. She looked you squarely in the eye without wavering as her steely blue eyes lingered fleetingly on yours. You felt alone. Each of us had been touched. And this was just attendance! It was a tool that I would use throughout my professional career to create the aura that learning was sacred and paramount above everything else. Her classes in English literature were not unique in terms of strategies, techniques, or gimmickry. They were unique because of her presence and we felt that what we were doing in that moment in time and space was important.

She addressed us as Mr. and Miss, and made us like the formality of being titled. The course concluded in June with the infamous New York State Regents Exam. Even the lowliest in her class strove to pass the exam. No one wanted to bear the identity of being a student who had failed this great lady's class. The sheer power of her presence and strength of her character had instilled within us the desire to succeed in spite of our own academic frailties. You didn't dare fail her course because in doing so, you failed her. The reader may conclude at this juncture that scaring hell out of kids is not the most positive method of influencing their development. But caution is advised because on the other side of the coin of fear is the word respect. We feared failure because we respected her too much to let her down. We knew that behind that mask of formality and dominance was a woman who cared for her brood. She was simultaneously our protector and our taskmaster. She made each of us feel that her mission in life was dedicated to the single premise of getting us to open our minds to the genius of Western literature. That's why we affectionately called her Ma when out of earshot and respectfully addressed her as Miss in her presence.

My chief regret as I look back on my life is that I never had nor did I take the opportunity to say, "Thank you." Without ever being consciously aware of their effect upon me at the time, these teachers managed by the sheer force of their character and the depth of their commitment to profoundly affect my vocational choice. In later years at about the midpoint of my career a critical event occurred which forced me to become more acutely aware of my role in the lives of my students and the effect that words had had upon the course and direction of their lives.

It happened during the Christmas shopping season. I was wending my way through the crowds of frustrated shoppers, when I became aware of my name being called out. As I looked around two nuns began to emerge from out of that morass of humanity and move directly toward me. They greeted me by name again and, as any teacher who has taught for any extent of time will tell you, I frantically searched through my memory's catalogue of faces for the name of these former students. They bailed me out. They were keenly aware of my obvious lack of recognition as well as perplexed at being accosted by two young women of the cloth. They quickly identified themselves as twin siblings who had been in one of my social studies classes at the school district where I initiated my career in 1960. Their next words left me dumbfounded and overcome by an emotion that I had seldom experienced—humility. They thanked me for being the person who had most influenced their decision to enter the holy orders. My response to this revelation was to lamely say, "Oh, I'm sorry!" They laughed; I cringed.

The discourse that ensued was somewhat one-sided and revealed that one of my presentations on life and its oft-times abbreviated sojourn for some, had touched these two impressionable eighth graders. I did not recall, even vaguely, my words or the class, but the two sisters, no pun intended, had their lives changed and directly influenced by me.

I believe that this chance meeting changed me and my perception of teaching. As a teacher I had made and would make hundreds, if not thousands, of presentations to students. Until that fateful day at the mall, I had not really been aware of the effect that a teacher could have on those tabula rasas sitting in front of me. Those two young people awakened me to the realization that words were more powerful than actions. I henceforth became more careful in the preparation and selection of my words; not because I was afraid of sending more students into a religious vocation, but because of my newly discovered powers to change and affect young peoples' lives.

To some readers this may appear as the epitome of arrogance. It is not. Every teacher worthy of the name is cognizant of the opportunity to make a difference. This factor, in my estimation, is the one that separates the truly good teacher from the mediocre practitioner. Wang Yang-Ming, a 14th century Chinese scholar-philosopher, summed it up perfectly when he stated, "To know and not to act, is not to know!" Those of us who have taught and know realize the power of a word or words; not those words said in anger or for praise, but those whose subtlety in the classroom is not lost upon a certain young woman or man or child who perceives that you are speaking directly to him/her at that precious moment in time and space. Yes, I wished I had personally thanked Prof, Coach, and Ma for being there and speaking those words to me. In some small way I would like to think that my thirty-three years before the mast was my thank you to them.

It would be stating the obvious to observe that teaching in those early days of my career, i.e., the 1960s and '70s, were somewhat unique. I could enumerate an extensive list of factors that have undergone a metamorphosis during four decades of pedagogical experience. But, in retrospect, it is my firm belief that the relationship between teacher and student has by far been the most affected. Every teacher that I came into contact with during my tenure shared at least one common factor that had motivated their decision to enter teaching—they liked kids and enjoyed being around them. For myself, it was the primary reason. I wanted to lead them, mold them, and watch them grow into confident, useful human beings and know that it was I who had been the architect of this creation. Although an Olympian assumption without doubt, it was tempered by that too often scarce commodity in our society today called caring. You will recall that I commented earlier in this chapter that those individuals who had been the primary influence in my vocational selection had projected the same identical characteristic, they cared about you as a person. And so it was with all of us, we liked them and we cared for them. There is a legal term in education law referred to as in loco parentis, i.e. "in the place of the parent." Although the law provides for extensive limitations on the exercise of this provision, to all of us it was a de facto reality. We cared for our charges and they were ours. Unfortunately, in recent years the currency of these two factors, liking and caring, have become debased.

This observation may startle and even anger some in the education community who will be quick to deny that teachers/administrators don't like or care for children. They will be defensive because they will perceive it as another weapon to be used by public education's enemies to further demean and criticize the profession. However, as was the habit of the ancient Greek philosophers who strolled through the Gardens of Academe in search of the truth, let us not deny it merely because it is unpleasant or leaves us vulnerable! It is the teacher's greatest challenge. We want to like these kids, and we do care for them, but within a delimited boundary. Due in large measure to statutory requirements and recent litigation, the liking and caring has become qualified and restrained and, sadly, the real casualty of the education wars.

The socio-economic revolution of the sixties was characterized, if I may be permitted to generalize, by the intensive interrogation of the raison d'être of any and all establishment bureaucracies. The educational establishment was not exempt from this inspection. Strangely enough, however, instead of the public school system being purged or circumscribed in its powers and jurisdiction, it was in fact endowed with an enhanced and, as it turned out, onerous responsibility. The school's formerly restricted forum was to be expanded into a de facto family of orientation wherein society's roll-call of problems—i.e., drug abuse, alcoholism, teenage pregnancy, alienation, racism, and violence—were to be treated and cured by the public school system.

The educational establishment in a messianic mind-set accepted the gauntlet. That cavalier-like decision, however, would carry a high price tag, namely the loss of public trust and confidence in the public school system when it proved in the public's perception to be ineffectual and incapable of producing a generation of socially, economically, and morally functional young men and women. It was inevitable that a former pillar of society whose dependability and performance had been relied upon without question would be placed in the docket as the accused defendant.

Teachers. What had happened to our teachers? Had the labor union movement polluted and distorted their mission? Could this role model of society be depended upon any longer to inspire and motivate our youth? Public complacency was now replaced by suspicion and a seeking of accountability for the so-called failure of our schools. The public's historical perception of the teacher, both culturally and economically, has generally been one of patronization and, as a class, relegation to the status of a second-class citizen. To many, George Bernard Shaw's epithet perfectly described and forever condemned the status of teachers to oblivion when he stated, "Those who can, do, and those who can't, teach!" Accompanying this devastating observation was what this author refers to as the Ichabod Crane syndrome. In it we see the somewhat effeminate image of the male pedagogue, skilled primarily at the weaving of tales, garbed in threadbare attire, and the object of derision by real men. Teaching was, and to many today is, not considered a manly vocation. Hence, it was considered women's work. Even today teaching is numerically dominated by females, with seventy percent of our teachers being women.

The gender issue, especially in public education, has always been the skeleton in the academic closet. The negative relationship existing historically in American society between socio-economic success and feminine gender was even more magnified by the Gothic image of the schoolmarm with the dismal specter of spinsterhood hovering over her. However, the pendulum swung at the end of the eighteenth century from that of a sectarian dominated view of public education's mission to a more secular model. The task for the instruction and preparation of America's youth was entrusted to that gender whose maternal and familial instincts were best suited to inculcate learning.

The drive to make teaching a true vocation, if not professionalize it, was initiated by men such as Horace Mann and Henry Barnard during the first half of the nineteenth century. Few of these educational statesmen trained in the law and/or ministry, had actually spent much time if any in a classroom as a teacher. Their primary concern was to ensure an orderly society by creating a conservative corps of dedicated and subservient teachers who would inculcate, if not indoctrinate, the habits of obedience, patriotism, and morality into their eager charges.[1]

Implicit within the shift towards universal, publicly controlled schooling was an assumption that was critical to the future philosophical foundation of American education. The family of orientation and simple community volunteerism, was no longer capable of sustaining and making the required progress necessary to the maintaining of a rapidly industrializing society. The socio-economic demands being made upon its collective members appeared to dictate that mandatory public education administered by a professional class of educators was now required. Many present-day critics of the public school system attack this decision when making their strained argument for returning the schools back to the family, i.e. the parents. But more on this later.

The Preparation and Training of Teachers

A much debated if not researched topic of controversy which forms the basis for much of the rhetoric regarding school reform is that of the training and preparation of teachers. Historically, until the watershed sixties, such training was generally conducted within an environment heavily influenced by the Prussian authoritarian model and more often than not in isolation from non-pedagogical students and disciplines. The normal schools in their earliest days, i.e., late nineteenth century, derived much of their curriculum from standard works on moral and psychological philosophy. These studies were largely reflective of secularized Protestant presuppositions accompanied with a sprinkling of Anglo-American philosophical realism. The pedagogical values encompassed norms of orderliness and in consort with a thorough mastery of basic mathematical and English usage.

Between 1910 and 1940, the transition from state normal school to state teacher's colleges took place. This change in titles was a substantive one reflecting the development of a four-year program based upon the successful prior completion of a recognized high school program and subsequent conferring of a baccalaureate degree. The new pedagogy of the progressive twenties began to demand that a teacher select her own instructional materials rather than follow a closely prescribed course of study and be capable of stimulating a student's intellectual interest(s) into more advanced stages of discover and analysis.

The post-war era witnessed a virtual inundation of research and development regarding the issue of teacher training and preparation. Triggered in most part by the 1983 publication of the now epic, if unchallenged, "A Nation at Risk," the conditions of environment for learning existing in the elementary and secondary schools were naturally linked to the conditions and circumstances surround teacher educa-tion., Furthermore it was observed by Zhixin Su's review of a century of education reform in teacher preparation that there was an almost complete failure to establish the teacher preparation process within either the context of exiting school systems or the ideal conception(s) of school(s).

There is no lack of research, studies, and theories regarding the training and preparing of individuals to enter teaching as a profession. The Achilles heel however in much of the research, of which this author does not claim total or near total familiarity, still founders on the rocks of the lack of consistent identification of individuals who will make the truly good teacher. Schools of Education in colleges and universities are confronted with the dilemma of attracting/retaining students in order to exist and the contending moral responsibility of informing and/or dropping an aspiring young man/woman from the program due to an inadequate capacity to perform effectively as a classroom teacher. This is the crux of the matter: Who do we as a nation allow to enter the classroom? How do we select, monitor, direct, cultivate, and finally graduate those among us who would lay claim to the title, teacher? Warm bodies and idealistic aspirations were sufficient to get by once upon a time, but not anymore.

This author would look for specific characteristics in a person who aspires to teach. These traits would emulate those of a military officer trained for a leadership role, knowledgeable in tactics/strategies, well-versed in human management techniques, and capable of quickly assaying an enemy's strengths and weaknesses. It would be an individual who has great survival instincts and who knows when to tactfully retreat as well as advance. The final ingredient, and perhaps the most critical to a teacher's survival and longevity, is the capacity to take s—t gracefully. The master teacher, both in the quality of performance and the extent of longevity of service, possesses this ability. The aforementioned fecal matter comes in a variety of forms and from diverse sources. The most frustrating aspect of this unsavory reality is that you, the teacher, cannot, except in a very limited number of instances, return the fire.

An analogy to the lotus blossom of Asian lore is certainly apropos. The lotus, considered in Asian myth to be the epitome of perfection and beauty, is borne and nurtured in the muck and mud of an oft-times malevolent environment. Its growth to maturity and perfection is, however, unaffected by its origins and in reality brings grace and beauty to all that it touches. As the plebe at West Point who must suffer for one year the slings and arrows of outrageous upperclassmen, so it is with the public school teacher. The only difference, and it is a considerable difference, is that the s—t never ends for the teacher.

As an example, let us look at the level of language used both in its volume and in its content within the halls of academe. I wonder how many other professional vocations must accept, if not tolerate, the R- and X-rated level of what passes for informal and generally normal conversation among students today. How many times a day, a week, or in a month, does the non-teaching professional get the opportunity to hear: f—k, a—h—e, scumbag (the nicest one), b—d, b—h, c—t, p—k, s—t, a—s, t—s, to name the most popular epithets. Mind you, now, these words do not get uttered in emotional situations alone but in ninety percent of the cases take place within the context of casual and normal pupil conversation.

The process, as I like to refer to it, is akin to the brutalization of the character of an inmate in one of Sohlzenitzen's Soviet Gulags. Unlike the inmates there, teachers are allowed to return home each day. The process is incremental, with the exponential factor increasing as one moves up through the grades. High school obviously is the greatest offender. The son et lumiere, i.e., sights and sounds, of the teacher's work day set the tone of the building and are hence absorbed into the teacher's psyche until, as in the gulag, what is abnormal on the outside becomes the norm on the inside. The unexpected becomes the expected and like a defensive auto-driving course one becomes conditioned to expect the worse and is suspicious and/or apprehensive when the opposite occurs.[2]

The aforementioned brutalization process has other casualties besides the teacher. Specifically, those students too often in the minority who have actually come to school to learn and who act and converse in a manner more appropriate to polite society. More, in a later chapter, will be devoted to these dispossessed scholars.

All other things being equal, the factors of perseverance, endurance, and depth of character are those factors which would weigh most heavily in the selection, training, and retaining of future teachers. This is not to say that intellectual capacity and ability to communicate effectively with students are to be minimized and assigned a subordinate role. What this author maintains is, simply, that in order to be an effective classroom teacher, an individual must possess the mental toughness of a military officer complemented by a Mother Theresa instinct for students and their ultimate well-being. Walking on water from time-to-time doesn't hurt either.

How do we go about attracting young men and women to enter a domain where angels fear to tread? It was common forty or fifty years ago that over ninety percent of those entering the teaching ranks would continue teaching until retirement or past it. Those who didn't especially males, went into the administrative stream. An unlimited source of neophytes, in the form of women could be depended upon to replenish the ranks. Not so today. The invigoration of the issue of gender equity in the workplace and in government, as well as home during the sixties, afforded a much broader choice of careers to women. Some schools of education closed down while those still remaining found themselves in an intense competition to attract entrants into their respective programs. In a sense this was a blessing in disguise because it forced the departments of education at these schools to self-examine critically what they had been doing and what changes would be necessary in order to remain solvent and prepare effectively a new generation of teachers. The results of this introspective examination have been mixed. On the one hand, the more recent influx of thousands of idealistic young men and women is strong evidence that teaching as a profession is still somewhat attractive. Programs for teacher training, with their concomitant philosophical foundations and associated objectives, have become fertile ground for the planting and cultivation of a variety of hybrid pedagogical reform movements.

This author, after reviewing some representative research on the subject of preparing and training individuals to become teachers, could not help but feel that in many instances the various education schools and their respective philosophies on teaching resembled in some ways the debate that at one time took place within the stage and movie industries between the method system of acting versus the natural school of acting. My reason for equating the two disciplines, teaching and acting, is that both require a performance before a critical, and more often than not, disinterested audience. Stated in simpler terms, can individuals be trained and prepared to enter classrooms by the systematic use of a vocabulary of responses specifically designed to solve or manage certain problems and/or conditions which normally occur within the school/classroom? There are numerous schools of education and educators who, with certain qualifications, endorse such a regimen of preparation. There are also those in the field who would immerse as quickly as possible the prospective pedagogue into the treacherous waters of a classroom environment.

It was this author's initial pedagogical experience to be assigned a class in elementary physical education no earlier than his undergraduate junior year, and for only six weeks. In my senior year, I was assigned an eight week stint in a semirural school district teaching physical education, K-12. That was the extent, along with a comprehensive background of various physical, health, and athletic curricula, of my preparation for the classroom. The issue of when and how to immerse the prospective pedagogue into a real classroom setting appears to revolve around two schools of thought with other theories being variations on the twin themes.

A number of educators, such as Dean Willis D. Hawley, of Peabody College, propose an accelerated classroom experience. They conclude that a strong liberal arts background in close association with course work on learning theory and teaching methodology, could be integrated into a program which would place future teachers in a classroom setting much earlier in their undergraduate careers.[3] This approach was in direct opposition to the Holmes Group and Carnegie Task Force on Teaching as a Profession Reports, which after completing research on prevailing teacher education programs of the 1970s and early '80s, advocated a more delayed approach. The gist of the latter was to support a plan which would eliminate undergraduate teacher education programs altogether and replace them with a comprehensive liberal arts program followed by a fifth year of education courses and cadet teaching concluding with the granting of a master's degree in teaching.[4]

It is an unfortunate but valid fact of academic life that the quest to create an individual who would be ready to assume the responsibilities and perform the task of effectively educating America's youth would be enmeshed in a parallel quest by teacher training institutions and faculties responsible to achieve acceptance and an academic status on a par with their professional counterparts in such fields as law or medicine. As stated previously in this chapter, the second class status of teachers and specifically, women, who taught young children in elementary schools resulted in the institutionalization of a professional inferiority complex.

Those graduates of law, medicine, and engineering schools have historically professed to know more than their clients. They work independently more often than not; possess a fixed and respected body of knowledge, and, in general, regulate their respective professions. In contrast to this image, teachers are generally perceived as being subordinate in their vocational pursuit. They are directed in their daily endeavors by so-called superiors in their field as well as by political institutions and personalities. Their training institutions present little continuity or agreed-upon disciplinary consensus. The public's perception of a directed-group requiring supervision and written instructions in order to perform their task(s) persists and is in all probability equally accepted, unfortunately, by too many in the profession.

Education Law 3012, for example, in New York State says it all when it states that tenured teachers, "shall hold their respective positions during good behavior and efficient and competent service, and shall not be removed except for...insubordination, immoral character or conduct unbecoming a teacher; ... inefficiency, incompetency, physical or mental disability, or neglect of duty..." It would be of interest to review, would it not, the provisions of the statutes throughout the country which govern the other professions, in order to see how many include insubordination and good behavior as criteria for retaining their respective licenses to practice their chosen vocations.

It was this atmosphere of subservience, in concert with authoritative sanction, that partially explains this author's involvement and total immersion in the union movement during the decades following the sixties. Ask any teacher what one of the biggest gripes and subtle insults to his/her status as a professional is and their unanimous response will be—the flood of administrative directives, regulations, FYIs, policies and suggestions that inundate them on a daily, weekly, monthly, and annual basis. The import of the message no matter how varied is always the same—'The teacher needs to be informed and directed as to how to proceed in the conduct of their chosen vocation. Remember, you hold your position tenure or not, for exhibiting '...good behavior...' and being 'subordinate.'"

So, you wanna be a teacher?

Notes

1.*Encyclopedia of Education, ed. Lee C. Deighton, Vol. 9, (New York: MacMillan Co. and Free Press, 1971), 71-73.*

2.*Alexander Solzhenisten, The Gulag Archipelago (New York: Harper and Row, 1974), 24-25.*

3.*Carolyn M. Evertsen, Willis D. Hawley and M. Zlotnik, "Making a Difference in Educational Quality through Teacher Education," Journal of Teacher Education, 36(3), 1986.*

4.*The Holmes Group, Tomorrow's Teachers (Lansing, Author, 1986), 30-33.*

5.*New York State School Boards Association, School Law, 27th ed., (Albany: New York State School Boards Association, Inc., 1988). 161-162.*

Chapter Two

Fellow Colleagues

2

Fellow Colleagues: Friend or Foe?

This chapter was probably the most difficult to compose. It was a challenge to my capacity to objectively portray teachers as individuals and as a class without having my personal and professional prejudices obscure the search for truth. Even as a child I was impressed and somewhat in awe of my teachers. Even as I progressed from childhood into adulthood, although tempered by maturity and experience, that somewhat lofty pedestal assigned to teachers remained intact. Perhaps it was my ethnic background and/or cultural environment which reinforced the occupation of teaching as being quasi-divine. Whatever the case, I can never recall not being strongly affected by the presence of a teacher or the environment of the classroom.

The closest association to the experience of formal education, both as a student and later as a teacher, was of a religious nature. Both then and now the classroom has always been the cathedral of my life's purpose. To enter the classroom as a student and be filled with the desire to seek out knowledge, and simultaneously be aware that your teacher not only shares but is prepared to lead you to that threshold of enlightenment has for me been the so-called high. It is the standard that many of my fellow colleagues and I use to measure the real worth and value of our profession. Whatever the interest, or better yet the disinterest, level of our oft-times reluctant scholars may be, it is essential that the teacher foster, create, and maintain an aura of immanence, if not eminence, at all times. The effective teacher must generate by reputation and consistent performance a reasonable facsimile of the so-called religious experience. By this we mean that the individual is transported spiritually from the known to the unknown. Through this process of revelation the individual is exposed to increasingly higher levels of awareness/consciousness until, as the historical Buddha experienced and as the ancient Greek philosophers sought, the moment of truth is at last attained. The teacher who cannot, or even worse will not, consistently make the attempt to breach the walls of student indifference does not belong in the classroom. The daily disappointment and frustration of being overtly jeered at, covertly reviled, or, even worse, ignored by those whom you would teach marks the Rubicon between the master teacher and the mediocre time-card practitioner.

There has always been and there will always be the student or students, class or classes, that make you want to call in sick and/or stimulate latent homicidal tendencies. It seems that no matter what strategies or approach you implemented, they were doomed to failure, the one word that no teacher can live with. And, tomorrow, at precisely the same time and in precisely the same manner, the nightmare scenario continues—Bill Murray's Groundhog Day lives. It is the master teacher who manages to keep his/her professional demeanor and approach their 'charges' as if each day was DAY ONE. It is the master teacher who conceals an increasing dislike to be in the presence of these contemptible monsters, treats them civilly and fairly despite knowing full well that there will be little or no reciprocation in kind. It is an experience akin to Dante's Inferno wherein the sinner is condemned to exist for eternity in his particular hell. The master teacher fights back with all the cunning and skill they possess. They know, however, that they will never make the conversion of the barbarian(s). But they never stop making the attempt and, like lemmings, rush to their doom[1].

Sometimes, but not very often, endurance and persistence result in a conversion and a soul is saved. These victories are few and far between. But, to the master teacher it has been well worth the travail. In this profession we maximize our victories and minimize our defeats. As a social science teacher or history teacher, a title I feel more comfortable with, the reader will have already become suspicious of a propensity on the author's part to make historical comparisons.

My early notions of the special if not sanctified status of the teacher were reinforced by my later professional immersion into world history, especially that of the Asian variety. The Asian tradition, particularly in India, Japan, and China, has tended more often than not, to evaluate the teacher almost to the point of deification. This is in stark contrast to the American tradition wherein almost the opposite opinion prevails. As a class, the teaching vocation is considered to be one of the most honored vocations in Asia. The guru of India, the sensei of Japan, and the Chinese Mandarin scholar have historically occupied a lofty status in their respective societies.

The definition of a teacher in the aforementioned cultures may be somewhat misleading, however, when compared to its counterpart in the United States. The vocation of teaching within the Asian context has historically been associated with that of a semi-religious calling. There the teacher by means of instruction, discussion, and questioning utilizes the content of the subject matter to cultivate and elevate the aspirations and character of his pupils. This process requires the teacher to be more than master of his subject matter. It requires that he be mentor, guide, advisor, counselor, chaplain, and confessor.

In Asia the search for and the recognition of truth has generally taken place within a sphere of transcendent universalism, wherein the master and the pupil seek out not only the meaning of their finite physical existence but their eternity as well. The expansion of the intellect of the individual so as to conduct one's life in harmony with nature and in accordance with a universal order cannot and must not be held inferior to the accumulation of so-called useful knowledge. It is at this point in the human drama that the teacher/guru/sensei becomes the most critical catalyst in a young scholar's education.

Gandhi understood it well. He reproached some of his fellow nationalists in the midst of India's independence movement regarding the use of brute force as a means to achieve independent status. He stated unequivocally that the world would judge India not by its success in achieving statehood, for that was inevitable, but in the manner and the process by which she would attain it. He knew that if the process does not ennoble the person then the consequent objective sought, despite its attainment, will be debased. This is the real challenge for the teacher in the modern era.

Over the years I have had the opportunity both to observe and evaluate fellow colleagues privately within a broad context of educational experiences and activities. I must caution the reader that when I use the word "evaluate" it is not used in the sense of a formal, written, administrative review to be placed in a personnel file. My evaluations are based upon informal observations and first-hand professional contact in a variety of settings, such as committees, seminars, workshops, and the like. Student commentary to a limited degree along with administrative sensing also afforded insights into the habits and character of the members of a school's instructional staff. What follows are composites of individual characters which portray faithfully it is hoped, the mosaic of the teaching vocation. It should be further noted that this author has attempted to remain objective and minimize his personal prejudices and predispositions which over four decades in the profession have had their accumulated effects on his opinions and beliefs.

PORTRAITS

The Disciplinarian or Benevolent Despot

This is the teacher who views the classroom as one's castle. The area directly adjacent to the room's entrance is the moat. The door is really a drawbridge which leads to the laird of the castle. Each student or peasant/serf has an assigned seat. Attendance is carefully taken and checked for AWOLs— those who have temporarily escaped from the manor. Instruction and assignments are straightforward with few gimmicks being utilized to make the classroom and/or assignments fun or enjoyable. Those scholars who have come to school with the primary aim of avoiding doing any work and/or raising hell hate this teacher, the period, and the subject with a passion. They will do anything including serve time in after-school detention in exchange for illegally cutting the dreaded class. Parents and administrators love this teacher. For the former it reminds them of the old days when you didn't get away with anything and the teacher was the boss. For the latter it makes the job of administering the building that much easier. And, easier is always better for the administrator.

This teacher more often than not is a male, although some of the toughest of this type have been women. Our despot usually perceives him/herself as a minority group engaged in a struggle not unlike David battling with Goliath. Discipline and learning are two sides of the same coin with one being unable to function without the other. The good students who actually come to school for an academic purpose will remember these teachers years later with a wry smile as they recall those days of fear, respect, and wonder. "Hail Caesar, We who are about to die, salute you!" will be words recalled from the pages of ancient history that seemed so apropos as they marched into that teacher's room. And they will tell their children about this teacher with an understanding borne of maturity, that they didn't die but, in fact learned something in that room and liked it.

The author must remind the reader that the term benevolent was not lightly selected to modify the word despot. A teacher who is a strong disciplinarian but unenlightened as to its true purpose is no better than a Mr. Brocklehurst as antagonist to Jane Eyre. To invoke a strict discipline in the classroom for no better purpose than to translate authority into manifest power is the basest of all pedagogical designs. The benevolent despot imposes a strict disciplinary environment upon one's charges for the primary purpose of instilling a sense of self-discipline that will permit the student to function successfully both in and out of the classroom. The undisciplined mind no matter how brilliant its owner will never fulfill its potential and hence deny itself and humanity the ultimate fruits of its genius. To any teacher there can be no greater dereliction of duty than failing to comprehend the real role of discipline and to exercise it to its maximum educational potential.

The Pal

In stark contrast to the authoritarian benevolent despot is the teacher who can't resist and, in most cases insists on, being a pal or friend to the entire student body. This teacher arrives at school each day with the purposeful enterprise of reaching-out and touching in the symbolic sense as many students as possible. You can identify this species quite readily. They will also be among the most popular teachers with the students. Those students who will gravitate towards this teacher are generally low or under-achievers, those who are discipline problems, those students who have home problems, and, in most cases, those youngsters who are lost in time and space.

This teacher, strangely enough, will probably not be a guidance counselor or athletic coach. The teacher who is a pal will allow if not insist on being called by his/her first name. The line between being a teacher and friend will be blurred if not eliminated. Certain expectations on the part of the students will ensue, such as passes being issued for the library, lavatory, lockers, cafeteria, and nurse's office, on demand. In return, our pal receives all of the inside information unavailable to his/her colleagues regarding what's really going on in school and at home. The students look upon this archetype as a real friend, superior to not only their other teachers but their parents as well.

Whereas his/her competitor, the authoritarian, will generally dress in shirt and tie, the students' friend will wear casual attire that more closely approximates that of the student body. Classroom demeanor and environment are also casual, with an atmosphere more approaching that of a cafeteria lounge. God help the teacher whose class follows the pal's class. The students will find it problematic to adjust to a more organized and disciplined atmosphere causing them to make the inevitable comparison between their pal and all other mentors who fail to meet his/her requirements. Guess who comes out smelling like a rose?

The pal does both good and harm to his/her charges. On the one hand he/she may very well be instrumental in saving a young man or woman from the disastrous circumstances of a dysfunctional personal, as well as, home life. By serving as a haven for lost souls who may obtain comfort and security in the knowledge that someone really cares, the friend of the student(s) provides an invaluable and oft-times crucial service.

On the minus side of the equation is the disturbing dichotomy which is created in the students' perception of the instructional staff. A friend versus foe mentality may, and often does, manifest itself. A teacher's value and expertise in the classroom is measure not in terms of efficiency, organization, and skill but in the coin of amity, familiarity, and fellowship. It is here that the real damage to the educational process takes place. The student has confused friendliness with effective teaching. Henceforth, any teacher who does not exhibit a friendly profile is labeled as a mean teacher who doesn't care for his/her pupils.

The negative attitude created by this too often misplaced veneration of friendship can have unfortunate consequences in terms of student/teacher communication. The opportunity for successful academic achievement and learning are rapidly diminished when the student's attitude towards a teacher or teachers is predicated on the thesis that, "He/she doesn't like me and isn't very friendly, so I'm probably going to fail!"

The Cultivator

Closely allied to the pal, but more often than not for differing reasons, is the cultivator. The cultivator must be observed carefully otherwise he/she will be mistakenly lumped into the pal class. On the surface this species of pedagogue will appear to assume the mantle of the pal. Beware, however, because the real purpose and intent of the cultivator, is to create an image and posture of friendship in order to win that most coveted of faculty designations and/or recognition the Most Popular Teacher award. However, the national penchant for being liked takes on a fascinating dimension when viewed within the context of the teaching profession. All teachers want to be liked by their students whether they admit it or not. It is one of the teacher's greatest fears to be disliked because he/she realizes the detrimental effect which such an atmosphere can have on the learning process. For the cultivator this fear becomes the sine que non for professional existence.

The cultivator makes contact with as many students as possible both in and out of the classroom, being careful to create the impression at being truly interested and concerned with each student's academic and personal life. He/she will almost always initiate the contact and ensuing conversation and while doing so will furtively search the halls for a new conquest. The cultivator, strangely enough, has little tolerance for the pal. Whereas the pal more often than not is a mediocre practitioner of the teaching art, the cultivator may be a good teacher with excellent abilities and organizational skills. In addition, he/she looks upon the pal as competitor for the hearts and minds of the student body.

The pinnacle of achievement for the cultivator arrives when he/she is designated in the senior yearbook as Most Popular Teacher or, even more euphoric, to have the yearbook dedicated to him/her with a photograph. This becomes a living memorial and is vindication of all the effort to raise a garden of devoted children.

The Minimizer or Angler

This species of pedagogue by nature is a practitioner of the art of doing as little as possible no matter what vocational choice is made. From the first day of their probationary appointment they have made a vocation of finding the easy way out with a minimum of effort. The minimizer will angle to obtain the easiest schedule of classes, with the last period free. They will make every attempt to avoid a homeroom and if they do not do so will probably shirk from being present at their assigned hall duty location. In the classroom they give the least quantity of assignments, complementing them with the lowest of expectations. Exams and assignments will generally be evaluated and returned a week or more after they were handed in by the students. The minimizer will be on a constant expedition to obtain from their fellow colleagues as many lesson plans, materials, and assistance that allow them to avoid doing their own research or development.

This breed is generally late for school or just makes it on time but is among the leaders in promptness and attentiveness to leaving the building at the specified time. The minimizers come in two distinct packages—almost totally unobtrusive to the point of being invisible or, much to the sardonic amusement of colleagues, using themselves as models to protest consistently at faculty meetings about the general lay public's ignorance and unappreciation for the laborious nature of teaching and the intensive effort necessary to be a good teacher.

The Mother Hen

This category is generally associated with the feminine gender but males have been successful in meeting the qualifications. Found primarily in the elementary and middle schools, as well as in English and Social Studies departments at the secondary level, members of this group achieve fulfillment of purpose both personally and professionally providing a nurturing and warm environment for their changes. The maternal instinct thrives and is raised to its fullest expression when the mother hen is with her brood. The legal term in loco parentis, "in the place of the parent," takes on its literal meaning by manifesting itself with the teacher attempting to recreate in the classroom the idyllic home away from home.

Though a stereotype at one time of the typical female teacher, especially at the elementary level, this species of teacher is a vanishing breed. As the technological revolution advances inexorably into our schools, the formerly personal, one-to-one relationship of the parent-teacher becomes invaded by a third party, the computer or machine. Students talk to machines; teachers talk to machines, teachers talk to students who talk to machines and the beat goes on. The mother hen is quite sensitive to this situation and with the knowledge that too many of her pupils or chicks originate from dysfunctional families compensates—some of her colleagues would say overcompensates—by performing the role of mother.

The female function is critical for the maintenance and

continuation of human society. That function which is shared by many sub-human species is the maternal instinct. It was the female's maternal instinct which the ancients in both the East and West, but especially in the East, recognized as a universal necessity. In India, the word "mata" means mother and also designates the cow, which by its labor prepares the earth for planting, moves the planting's bounty to home and market, and ultimately with its manure enriches the mother Earth. In China, the character for female, when joined with the character for son/child, gives rise to the word for good. Again, when the female character is combined with that symbolizing a roof over her head, the designation means peace.

Earth historically has been given a feminine identity and closely associated with the womb and henceforth, fertility. The nurturing factor in this continuing universal drama is self-evident. As with the ancients, many of us in the education enterprise realize that the process of learning is as crucial to shaping our youth as is the substance of what they learn. An individual's need to experience reliable and consistent support and succor is necessary to one's existence. If not, then the Hobbesian projection, that life under certain conditions becomes "...short, nasty and brutish..." may become one step closer to reality. Enter our mother hen.[2]

Given the current gender sensitive climate which pervades our society and construes any personal, physical proximity with a sexually exploitive connotation, the mother hen has become an endangered species. The hug, the pats on the head or shoulder, and the wink have all taken on dark and sinister meanings. The result of American society's joust with the devil has been, in the American classroom, the demise of that idiom which once defined the teacher/student relationship— love. The love of learning, the love of seeking the truth, the love of kids, their mentors forming a community of seekers of knowledge, and the love of saying, "I understand!" The social intimacy so critical to this process is no more. Like Margaret Mitchell's epitaph to the ante-bellum South, it has "Gone with the wind!"[3]

The Complainer or "Bitcher"

This genus is unhappy with life in general. They spend most of their waking hours finding fault with everyone and everything. Their unhappiness in school more often than not finds its source in a form of disillusionment with the progress of their careers. In many cases the classroom has become a trap wherein their frustration(s) becomes identified with poor student behavior and performance. Their original assumptions and teaching ambitions have come to naught and many consider themselves to be second class citizens because they are teachers. Most complainers are veteran teachers who never got out when they should have. Instead, they have accepted their subordinate status in society and have rationalized that the gods have conspired against them. Their job security, due to tenure and position on the salary schedule, has made them immune to any thoughts of escape.

The complainer can and does find something wrong with the administration, fellow colleagues, the student body, the Board of Education or School Committee, parents, secretaries, janitors, monitors, the building, curriculum and their schedules. Have we left anything or anyone out? Fridays and vacation periods are eagerly looked forward to as is the end of the school day. These complainers are among the first staff members to leave the building and for one reason or another are seldom available to assist students after school.

Complainers are all over the "lot" when it comes to efficiency and effectiveness in the classroom. The good ones do their job but don't ask them to do anything else. The rest cross over into the minimizer's domain.

The complainers' only solace is when they have a forum or audience, such as faculty or union meetings, and can publicly submit a staggering list of subjects with which they are dissatisfied. The crowning point of their day or week comes when they perceive that they have made a lot of people as unhappy with school as they are.

The Ambitious One or the Climber

This category is one of the author's favorites since in so many instances it has reinforced the validity of the Peter Principle. It has been fascinating over the years to observe the cast of players who entered the teaching profession with the purpose of making the classroom their stage but instead shifted their career direction and perceived that the role of administrator was in truth their real calling. The reasons for making such a decision differ but generally can be identified as variations on a theme based on the following trilogy: salary differential, escape from the classroom, and the inclination toward the status of educational leader. Teachers who, as when Billy Graham exhorts the multitudes to "...make a decision for God..." will either be motivated by a single component of the trilogy or a combination thereof.

It has been the author's experience that in observing those who have moved out of the teaching ranks and into a supervisory/administrative role have done so because of a perception that their talents, in association with the reasons stated in the aforementioned triad, are somehow greater than the role of mere classroom teacher. They feel that the confinement of the classroom is stunting their growth and development as an educator, a term that they definitely prefer once their professional transformation has been achieved.

Whether it's a by-product of this metamorphosis or a segment of the ambitious one's subconscious psyche, the climbers tend to forget their roots. They proceed to a posture towards fellow colleagues which signals the failing of this breed: condescension and superiority. Their perception of the profession's hierarchy and the reaffirmation of the correctness of their career decision rests on the assurance that teachers are at the bottom of the pecking order. Therefore, they reason, real career growth can only take place by escaping the classroom and committing to the climb up the educational corporate ladder.

As Shakespeare described Cassius in Julius Caesar, having a "...lean and hungry look..." so it is with our climbers. They are constantly on the prowl for any notice or rumor that an impending administrative or quasi-administrative position is about to open. In order to qualify for any such supervisory position(s) these people have had to enroll in and successfully complete a required course of study leading to a certificate. Another qualification not required by law, but a de facto prerequisite, nevertheless, is the talent to curry favor with and ingratiate oneself with the administrative powers that be, mainly principal, chairperson, supervisor, superintendent, or Board of Education.[4]

An excellent and proven course of action is to combine a zealous pattern of volunteerism along with vociferous support of all administrative initiatives and pronouncements. This combination of high profile activity will result in a definite tendency for the current administrative bureaucracy to look upon such people with increased favor.

Following such an unsolicited demonstration of assistance and support, climbers must move in a timely fashion to schedule a private/personal meeting with that administrator deemed to be most crucial to the successful attainment of their ambitions. Although this author has never been privy to such a meeting, experience, observation, and discussion with those who have undergone the transformation lend credence to a scenario not unlike that of the confessional. The sinners, i.e. our climbers, confess to the ecclesiastic authority, i.e., administrator, that they have come to the recognition of the error of their ways, namely, that the limited experience of the classroom has caused a crisis in their attitude and/or performance as an educator. The confession then enters the entreaty phase wherein our sinners seek guidance, advice, and encouragement as to their desire(s) to enter the cloister of the administrative sanctuary—mea culpa, mea culpa, mea maxima culpa.

The ambitious climbers in too many instances have been good teachers. It has been a sad and unrelenting tale of woe to observe over the years as highly successful classroom teachers leave that environment for the Olympian heights of administration. Prior to the unionization of the teacher corps the reason was primarily economic. Young men with growing families (65 percent of principals in 1990 were male) saw the administrative realm as an escape from a permanent state of penury. However, both prior and subsequent to the advent of nationwide legislation permitting the recognition and organization of unions in the public sector, the stereotypical ladder to academic success/achievement has led out of the classroom, not into it.[5]

The system has historically rewarded migration from the

classroom into the principal's or supervisor's office. Status has and is associated with vertical movement in juxtaposition to administrative stratification. This perception is classically illustrated in the discipline of physical education, wherein a physical education or gym teacher is expected and encouraged to follow the yellow brick road consisting of classroom (gymnasium) teaching and coaching, advancement to Athletic Director/Supervisor, then onto Assistant Principal and eventually to Principal. A few have even made it to the Superintendent's Office.

In retrospect, the educational establishment which includes teachers, appears to be overly impressed by titles. I believe this is true at all levels of education. This obsession, if I may call it such, with titular identification being synonymous with pedagogical achievement/success goes beyond the schoolhouse, infecting the general public as well. It was the author's personal experience to observe first-hand this phenomenon, especially at family gatherings during the holiday season. Those members of our extended family, i.e., cousins, uncles, aunts, grandparents, who had not had much contact with yours truly, would, during the course of polite conversation inquire into my vocational status. Upon hearing that after twenty years I was still just a teacher in the public schools, it became fascinating to observe their combined non-verbal surprise and disappointment that such a promising scholar had not achieved a higher status in education, i.e., administrative identity. I was then treated to a litany about my peers who had also entered the educational arena and had become administrators. My reaction to their commentary was unnerving (as it was meant to be) to say the least. I boldly proclaimed my total lack of ambition to become a principal, an office which for some reason carried great prestige in their minds. The conversation generally ended or the subject was switched to the volatility of the weather.

To this day, I firmly believe that in the eyes of my family, including my parents, that my passion for the classroom was interpreted as a lack of ambition and desire to achieve distinction in my chosen field of endeavor. An earned doctorate from New York University made little difference since the word doctor was almost solely associated in my hometown with that of a physician. I am afraid that I lacked the ingredient necessary for educational success: mountaineering. A "climber" I was not.

The Special Educator or Martyr

This is an interesting species to say the least due in large measure to the stark contrasts that exist among its members. Those individuals who attempt to pursue a career in special education share at least one characteristic in common—a messianic mission to liberate their pupils from the bondage of their physical and/or psychological limitations. The good ones quietly go about their jobs without seeking notoriety and along the way positively affect and improve the quality of life for their charges.

The burn-out factor in education which too seldom is taken into account by the general public is notoriously evident in special education. Too many of the good special education teachers leave either the discipline and/or the profession due to its intensity and emotionally draining features. The teacher want-ads both in the regular newspapers as well as professional journals consistently list more special education openings than almost any other discipline. The availability of positions is a primary reason for an increasing number of teachers to become dually certified in both their primary vocational choice and in special education which affords them an insurance policy of sorts during sparse budgetary periods.

Unfortunately there also exists within the special education ranks the martyr whose apparent aim in both their lives is to constantly publicize the difficult if not heroic efforts that they make on a daily basis in order to save or rescue their clients from Kipling's "...dread Egyptian night..." They delight in proclaiming, especially in faculty meetings and parents back-to-school nights, the many obstacles they encounter in a normal school day. The facts that their class sizes are one-third to one-half the size of the regular classroom teacher, that through the ever-burgeoning process of inclusion and mainstreaming they have generally less organized classroom contact than regular classroom teachers, and that the time-consuming correction of papers/projects/tests is considerably less is not lost on the sensibilities of their fellow colleagues. The undisguised contempt that most of the non-special education teachers share for the martyr sometimes erupts in an acrimonious debate that further widens the schism that already exists.

A typical day for our saviors, especially at the secondary level, includes socializing, testing, and providing an environment for such designated students that will allow their self-esteem to be either established and/or reinforced in a positive manner. Much of the day is spent visiting the regular classroom teachers in order to inquire about the progress or lack thereof of their mainstreamed charges. If the martyrs are clever enough they will manage to have their assigned charges included within the regular school program for most of the workday. However, such an eventuality can pose a problem namely, how to give the appearance of being involved in productive work and not being observed visiting the cafeteria or faculty room too many times.

There appears to be an inverse relationship in terms of degree of difficulty and/or problems, between secondary and elementary levels of special education instruction. Based upon observation, discussion, and eavesdropping, it would appear that the younger the student the greater becomes the intensity and effort which the special educator must exert in order to reach the child/student effectively. Being a martyr at the elementary level may be excusable but at the secondary level totally intolerable.

The Substitute (Per Diem)

If you want to know what's going on in your school(s) in terms of what's right and what's wrong with them, all you have to do is ask any competent per diem substitute. They will tell you who the best administrators and teachers are as well as the buildings and districts with the most and least discipline. They are, without fear of contradiction, the most effective tool that currently exists for evaluating a school system, a school building, a department, or a classroom. No high salaried consultant(s) and/or educational departments at the college or university level can appraise and gauge the substantive and procedural effectiveness of a school faster and more accurately than your lowly substitute teacher.

Who is this best kept secret and why does this author simultaneously render to them an inferior pedagogical status but a superior status as evaluator? In most cases, this afterthought in our educational line chart of authority and importance is generally a certified teacher who either voluntarily or

in most cases involuntarily does not hold a fulltime appointment. Substitutes can be retired teachers who seek additional income or have yet to cut the umbilical cord to their former
professional existence. In many instances they are newly
graduated and have been unable to obtain either a full or
part-time position in their field of endeavor. Their compensation is illustrative of their perceived importance in the educational hierarchy, they are paid considerably less than a
plumber, electrician or UPS delivery man's wage. Yet, and
herein lies the most hypocritical judgment made by school
authorities, they are expected on a moment's notice to
appear in a building/classroom, acquaint themselves within
minutes with the teacher's lesson plan(s) and schedule, as
well as the subtleties of the entire school's procedures. Hold
on, the best part is yet to come. They are actually expected
to teach the day's activities as if the regular instructor was
present. All this for an average of $45-60 a day!

Imagine if you will, psychologically preparing to undergo
a surgical operation or about to have a tooth drilled or go on
trial for your life, and at the last minute your regular practitioner, due to personal circumstances, is incapable of being in
attendance. In their stead a substitute has been designated.
Would you be mildly interested in this person's qualifications,
training, and background? Your expectations or at least your
assumptions would be that he/she is a certified, experienced,
and capable practitioner of the respective vocation. Should
we expect less of anyone who serves in "place of the parent"
(in loco parentis) and of the regular teacher in our schools.

The role of the substitute teacher in terms of frequency
and responsibility of performance has changed radically in
the last quarter century. The school authorities, like Dickens'
Pip, have great expectations. The money, recruitment, and

preparatory provisions for such expectations which are allotted by the same authorities are somewhat less in dimension. As some teachers grow older and take greater advantage of sick and/or personal leave and others take time to have and raise children, not only the desirability but the necessity of having a readily available pool of qualified and effective substitutes becomes mandatory.

Substitute teachers in states such as New York have already been organized and represented by public employee unions. The unions bring to the collective bargaining table a list of demands which in the past have been ignored or treated cavalierly by school districts. An intelligent and visionary administration would counter-organize this critical segment of the instructional staff by treating it collectively and individually with the professional courtesy and attention it deserves.

If I was a superintendent of schools I would see to it that, first, an organizational meeting of the pool of substitutes would be held in late August or early September. This meeting would include refreshments and serve as a conduit for the District to discuss its programs, goals, and educational philosophy. The substitute teachers, especially those with experience both within and outside of the system, could share their observations and possible recommendations regarding the District's rules, procedures, and program(s). Work among the substitutes, many of whom work in multiple districts, would soon get out that a certain district not only pays well but treats you as an integral and valued part of the system. Can the reader think of a better way to attract and maintain a dependable and efficient pool of substitute instructors while at the same time having possession of an invaluable source of objective evaluation? Of course, the real beneficiary of such an approach would be the students whose instruction at the desired levels of quality would be constantly maintained.

The Union Activist

Since the dawn of the Age of Enlightenment, which was 1967 in New York, when public employees were rescued from the Stone Age by a millionaire's son, Nelson Rockefeller, a new breed of teacher emerged from its long incubation period, the union activist. Two centuries of voluntary servitude especially on the part of the female teacher were finally and irrevocably brought to a shattering end. The silent frustration and experience with a historic public hypocrisy where the importance of good education was extolled by those who treated its purveyors with condescending contempt resulted in an outburst of demands for equity and redress.

This author will deal with the union movement as well as labor-management relations since 1967 in a later chapter. Suffice it to state that our interest at this point is to describe those individual teachers who for a number of personal and professional reasons took it upon themselves to lead Pharaoh's slaves out of bondage.

The early years of the union movement brought forth individual leaders who were coincidentally the natural leaders in their respective building, department, and/or discipline. Generally, they were elder statesmen and women with a few young Turks messing for a fight. They were idealistic and possessed with a powerful sense of mission. As the union movement matured and became more institutionalized, the motivations and attitudes of its leadership at the national, state, and local levels proceeded through a similar metamorphosis. A few of the original players on the teachers' side of the labor-management equation were in for the short term, their mission being to get the whole thing started and then grace-fully bow out in Deist fashion. They would serve in later years as model Founding Fathers and Mothers, recounting the early days of the revolution to younger audiences who whether willing or unwillingly were obliged to listen. It is to those who both inaugurated and actively continued the struggle in a leadership role that we are concerned with at this juncture.

Those teachers who led and continue to lead, especially at the local level, were and are faced with the delicate proposition of balancing their teaching vocation with their avocation, union activism and leadership. This balancing act which is uniquely associated with the teaching profession has resulted in a number of instances wherein a blurring or rever-sal of the distinction between the roles has occurred.

As an illustration, assume that we have a teacher who has become frustrated by any combination of professional bore-dom, student behavior, administrative prerogative, and/or perceived teacher apathy. This same teacher occupies a leadership role of president, negotiator, or grievance chair-person within his or her union. In seeking an avenue to vent frustrations, management windmills become the perceived enemy and the causative agent of misfortune to be tilted with at every opportunity. Like the muckraker in Pilgrim's Progress, nothing is left untouched or overlooked in the never-ending search for management misdeeds. For this type of activist, confrontation and adversarial relations are the name of the game. Compromise is considered to be a fatal weakness akin to almost being labeled a Quisling.[6]

Counter to the muckraker there exists that individual within the leadership whose initial response to perceived management misconduct is to find a common ground for both parties to achieve a rapprochement of sorts in order to achieve mutual satisfaction. This method of course involves the art of compromise and the dangerous but at times valuable utilization of the quid pro quo technique. A failure to reach a mutually beneficial outcome between the parties is considered by this activist to be deadly to sound labor-management relations. The failure to reach bilateral agreement means that recourse to a third party mediator/arbitrator becomes necessary. This can result in an individual with no vested interest in the two party's relationship rendering a decision which will alter and/or rearrange terms and conditions of employment.

The progressive activist sees failure not in winning or losing grievances but in the mere fact that both parties are forced to use such a process. The numerical frequency of third party intervention on an annual basis may be indication of an attitude held by either the Union and/or the District which prevents them from communicating as equals.

Teacher unions more often than not find their membership having to choose between the politics of confrontation and that of rapprochement. Having personally gone through both stages of activism, I can recommend without qualification the latter as the most advantageous in the long run to both labor and management. The activist who constantly seeks a common denominator for the settlement of issues realizes that you don't have to have a revolution in order to be revolutionary. The confrontation-oriented activist who revels in the revolution cannot see the destructive effects on future labor/management relations. The use of the quid pro quo to settle future disagreements can become severely damaged, rendering meaningless the give-and-take attitude so necessary for positive employer-employee relations.

Being a firm believer and advocate of the adage which allows an opponent all the rope they need to hang themselves, it is critical that a qualified trust between the union and the Administration be established and that both parties enter into a reciprocal relationship based upon mutual respect and equality. Much depends upon the individual agendas and egos of the personalities involved. Unions should be wary of the activist leaders dually bent on neutralizing the authority of the administration and delivering their people in messianic fashion from the evils of school superintendents and Boards of Education. Such leaders tolerate little, if any, disagreement with their actions from the membership and tend to perceive others within the ranks as in dire need of direction and leadership. Their modus operandi is to take minor issues and escalate them to a crisis status in order to reinforce their image as defenders of the right while forcefully denouncing the District's continued attempts to emasculate the Union.

The Jock

The jock's raison d'être is athletics/sports. All of life's events and its impact on our collective existence share a single, common denominator—the athletic contest. No matter what the topic under discussion may be, the jock will quickly and deftly reroute the conversation so that it takes on the dimension of and is equivocated with some sports event, person, skill or act which completely explains the cause and effect of the original topic under discussion.

The reader is cautioned not to jump to the conclusion that the author is singling out physical educators for special attention. Although many, but not all, physical education (P.E.) teachers fall into the caricature of the preceding paragraph, due recognition must be made of the contributions of those mostly males and a few females who occupy positions in the so-called academic disciplines. The non-P.E. areas that dominate the world of jockdom have historically included social studies (its premier source) and English. For some reason that I have never quite comprehended it has been a phenomenon that social studies teachers seem to have a genetic factor which tends to involve them in coaching athletics. It would be a mildly interesting project to research the number of social science teachers who at one time were involved or are presently involved in the coaching ranks.

Coaching a sport for both P.E. and non-P.E. instructional staff is the essence of their existence. This is obvious in the case of the P.E. teacher. Very few P.E. teachers look upon the classroom, the gym or field as their real vocation. It is coaching that makes them tick. The never-ending quest for the Holy Grail of sports, the undefeated season, is omnipresent. Such an achievement, especially if it is accomplished more than once, qualifies its architect, the coach, for communal canonization and possible professional advancement as an administrator. The notoriety and status which our nation assigns to winning and its most winning coaches increases exponentially the time, energy, and resources devoted to the athletic endeavor. For the P.E. teacher, it is win or be banished to the dreaded world of intramurals.

While the plight or condition of the P.E. teacher is readily understood, that of the non-P.E. classroom teacher is somewhat more complex. The teachers who coach and are not P.E. majors do it primarily because they once played the sport(s). They more often than not refrained from majoring in P.E. or Health in college due to its low status within academia. When their playing days were over the jock academicians turned to coaching as an outlet to their athletic energy and/or motivation. Their energy and desire to succeed as active participants is transferred into the minds and bodies of their adolescent charges. In some cases, the vocational choices of the non-P.E. jocks becomes blurred with the avocation of athletics. The last period bell is the clarion call to freedom from the perceived tedium and confinement of the classroom and the subsequent reincarnation as coach. The capacity to meet the mental and physical challenges of balancing the two arenas of academics and athletics becomes an onerous burden, especially as the years pass. The pressures placed professionally and domestically can be and often are a cause for early burnout.

Miscellany

There are other varieties of the teaching corps that come to mind. There is the women's right feminist, usually with a hyphenated name to preserve her identity, who is super-conscious of her gender. This feminist either overtly or more often than not covertly seeks to inculcate her ideals into the minds of her female charges by denigrating the male species wherever and whenever the situation allows.

There is the scholar or guru, usually a male, who takes every opportunity to inform his audience (he is in constant dread of not having one) of the subtleties or hidden meaning that exist in whatever topic or subject is under discussion. He will use the word "obviously" to infer that any real-thinking individual, such as himself, would have been able to discern the real issue(s) and/or fact(s) in the discussion as he obviously did. Faculty meetings and opening day sessions in September are the particular forums he chooses to enlighten his more obtuse colleagues. For new teachers who are unaware of his self-anointed status he can be readily identified by his stoop-shouldered and somewhat unsteady gait that is accompanied by a look of other-worldliness.

Not all teachers can be placed in a pre-selected category. Many teachers are too busy developing and perfecting their expertise in their vocational disciplines. Simply speaking they do their job and do it well. Their personalities, ideals, opinions, and/or prejudices are kept to themselves. In some ways they are a mystery to their students and fellow colleagues who have trouble fitting them into a niche. They are seldom quoted or spoken of by students who hold them slightly in awe. They are indeed the Scarlet Pimpernels of education. Thank God!

Notes

1 . Dante Alighieri, The Divine Comedy, ed. Frank N. Magill, (New York: Harper and Row, 1989), 194-198.

2 . Thomas Hobbs, Leviathan, (London: Dutton, 1973). 104.

3 . Margaret Mitchell, Gone with the Wind, (New York: Avon, 1973), 2.

4 . Leonard F. Dean, Twentieth Century Interpretations of Julius Caesar, (Englewood Cliffs: Prentice-Hall, 1968), 114-115.

5 . United States Department of Education, Schools and Staffing in the United States: A Statistical Profile (Washington, D.C.: Government Printing Office, 1993), 98.

6 . John Bunyon, Pilgrim's Progress, (London-New York: Dent, 1973), 54-55

Chapter Three

The Board of Education

3

The Board of Education: Stewards or Wardens?

Why the hell would anyone want to run for and become a member of a Board of Education (B.O.E.) or school committee? The financial remuneration is zero or less. Meetings, inclusive of regular, subcommittees, PTAs, Parent open houses and budget hearings and workshops to name a representative few impose a staggering burden upon the conscientious citizen board member whose obligation to family life becomes marginalized. Public monitoring of Board actions and deliberations can too often become ugly and personal as certain citizens and/or coalitions within the school district use Board meetings and members as fodder for their agendas and perceived grievances. The list is longer but the message is clearly sufficient to make the would-be candidate wary to the point of reconsideration.

In the four decades during which I served as both a teacher and union activist, I experienced what I believe to be a representative spectrum of the types of personalities and philosophies which could be found in most school districts throughout the state if not the nation. The reader must keep in mind at all times that the five to nine persons comprising a B.O.E. will take on at some point, a collective identity. This collective identity, analogous in some respects to a Grand Jury, will result more often than not in a school board with a persistent coincidence of mutually arrived at conclusions. In those school districts which contain strong Machiavellian personalities with purposeful agendas, the collective identity will not be left to chance.

Boards of Education, like the schools they have been given stewardship over, are a reflection of the communities and/or neighborhoods they represent. As the public's perception and conception of their schools change, so will the character of their elected/appointed School Committee or B.O.E. This change is often cyclical being similar in many respects to the classic Keynesian model of prosperity, recession (decline), depression (trough) and subsequent recovery. Keynes warned economic policymakers and others in authority that the cycle could get stuck at its lowest point, the trough, and that extraordinary means such as government intervention would be required to move the system back towards prosperity.[1]

Although the Keynesian model was obviously developed as an economic prototype it does offer some thought-provoking implications for school governance at the B.O.E. level. The major exception, and it is contingent to an entire school system's future growth and progress, is the substitution of the tax-paying public as surrogate for Keynes' public sector, i.e., government, interventionist role. As Keynes the economist sought to utilize the public sector to rectify any downturns in the economy and propel it towards its full growth potential, so can a community through its elected representatives maintain and expand the quality of its educational investment.This author makes what some may consider to be a dangerous assumption and that is: at present, the greater majority of American citizens continue to remain faithful to and advocates for public school education. I believe this presumption to be a valid one despite the current volume of criticism as well as outright condemnation of the American public school system. Unfortunately, many individuals of prominence and authority in both the pubic and private sectors are conspiring to dismantle and parochialize history's finest egalitarian educational design under the guise of school reform.

When the Japanese emerged from almost two and a half centuries of self-imposed isolation and created a modern nation-state in the mid-nineteenth century, their leaders recognized the necessity of a unified and centrist oriented citizenry. To those ends the Japanese leadership understood that the primary agency for forging a strong, united and purposeful nation-state would be a centrally-controlled public educational system. The educational system that they selected to emulate in terms of its organization and popular base was the American school system. Although the goals of the Meiji Government were different from our own, i.e., an obedient, educated, and loyal citizen to the Imperial throne, the procedure for obtaining same was a compulsory, free public school system.[2]

It is precisely this issue that is at the core of the current debate over the direction and organization of our public schools. The extensive and prolific verbiage being expounded by a variety of recognized authorities and experts in too many instances obfuscates the real issue: Whether the United States has the motivation and the will to commit the resources necessary to foster an egalitarian public school system or the public is to be offered a smorgasbord of fragmented institutions fostering a potpourri of philosophical sectarian goals. If it is the latter, then God help us because it will most assuredly lead to the disintegration of a United States of America and push the clock back to those antebellum days where we were *these* United States but not *the* United States.

For those who argue for freedom of choice in the selection of educational institutions, a warning—you may get what you deserve. The idealistic but unrealistic perception that school choice supported by public tax dollars will create a competitive and henceforth superior educational environment is a false prophecy. It will lead to the same conditions that existed prior to the Civil War when the several states considered their priorities to be paramount and those of the nation subordinate. We could afford the luxury of a Civil War in 1861 to decide the issue of Union. We were bordered on the north and south by two benign, underdeveloped states, Canada and Mexico. On the east and west were two great oceans which offered considerable insulation from foreign intrigue in our domestic relations. Our population in 1860 is estimated at 31 million, of which almost 13 percent was slave.

All this has changed. Today, we are a nation of over 285 million inhabitants. Technology has minimized the geographical insulation factor to virtual non-existence. We have become, as all people have become on planet Earth, global citizens. It is, therefore, incumbent upon us as a people to reflect upon, in a non-isolationist manner, the organization, philosophy, and performance of those nations' education systems who are our economic and/or political competitors. Almost to a nation these countries—Japan, France, England, South Korea, Taiwan, Israel and Germany—endorse and follow a nationally oriented curriculum with a strong central government role. In order to compete effectively and continue America's leadership on the world stage, our Boards of Education must confront and in a collegial manner engage in constructive dialogue at the regional/national level in order to fashion the schools of the 21st century.[3]

This daunting task will summon forth both the best and unfortunately the worst in our communities. As this author has previous stated, Boards of Education are cyclical in their character. Before the 1960s this cyclical nature was a luxury which we could afford. It no longer is. Our school systems cannot, in alternating periods often extending from three to five years, move from growth to decimation or stagnation. Too much in our social, political, and economic makeup depends upon what happens in our schools. Although schools cannot change society, they can and do effect the ideas and direction of individuals, i.e., students. Overseeing and directing through its policymaking function, the Boards of Education today more than at any other time in America's brief history perform a most critical role in guaranteeing the preservation of American sovereignty and global leadership. This responsibility to the nation is counterbalanced by the obligation of the Board member to see that the local community's needs, not necessarily its desires, are met.

Herein lies the Shakespearean rub—the necessity for national standards versus the immediacy of parochial demands. It is a task which mandates that the incumbent Board member enter an environment where angels fear to tread. The qualifications for such an office are, to quote a popular adjective, awesome. The individual must possess a Gandhian strength of commitment and perseverance that does not wither under fire or criticism as well as retain an objectivity that allows for all viewpoints to be equitably considered. It may very well take a Mahatma to do the job! It is a difficult standard to achieve; many would say impossible. As Lincoln earnestly pleaded in his first inaugural address to a divided nation that, "...the better angels of our nature..." prevail, so to for our Board members. In certain respects the issues of division remain the same—race, regionalism, and national sovereignty. There is one great institutional difference, however, between that fractious era and today and it is an institutional difference that can be decisive in avoiding another such cataclysmic event or in fostering it. That institution of course is our public schools.[4]

We previously stated that schools do not change society, but they can powerfully effect the content and direction of its clients. It is these clients who will change society. How the family, neighborhood, nation, and globe are perceived by young people is pretty much a result of their personal and formal educational experiences. And who is it that sits in the highest position of authority in the local pyramid of educational hierarchy? It is, of course, the B.O.E., stewards of our schools and oligarchical proprietors of its mission.

Depending on the individuals that comprise a B.O.E., the mission of a school district will more often than not reflect the political, religious, and/or philosophical predisposition of its individual members. With this in mind, a compilation of vignettes of individual types of Board members who this writer has observed and interacted with over the course of four decades follows.

The Fiscal Watchdog

This breed, a.k.a. the fiscal conservative, is found on every Board of Education in every school district in America. To a certain extent, the Fiscal Watchdog (FWD), is necessary to a balanced functioning of any B.O.E. Their whistle-blowing nature assures that the educational powers-to-be consider carefully any proposal with fiscal implication that is presented to the Board. Their motto is, "If it's fiscally sound, it's educationally sound!" Over the years only two such members of the Board of Education that I observed were ever primarily interested in the educational program.

In the overwhelming majority of the cases, the fiscal conservatives, either singly or as the representative of a taxpayers group, are concerned solely with the tax rate on their real estate holdings. Since the incremental size of the annual school budget is generally related to an increase in the tax rate, the FWD's principle raison d'être is to either freeze, reduce, or that failing, to grudgingly accept a miniscule increase in the annual budget. Those FWD's who cannot absolutely accept any increase will vote no on the annual budget and then proceed, for the sake of the media in attendance, to go into a lengthy dissertation explaining their courageous act in the face of a spend-thrift majority.

Fiscal Watchdogs will blame in descending order their fellow Board members, administrators, the teacher's union, local and state governments as the reason for increasing the burden on the local homeowner. They will raise, as the focal point of their dissent, the grim specter of the elderly being evicted from their homesteads where generations of family were domiciled due to a default on their school taxes. This of course will cause many in the audience to shudder, although practically no one, if any, have ever known of such a circumstance in their local school district.

If FWD's are a minority on the Board, then the effect and/or damage rendered is minimized. If, however, the alternative is a reality and a majority of the Board are in the FWD's camp then as Bette Davis offered in All About Eve, "Fasten your seatbelts, it's going to be a bumpy night." Each member of the FWD camp or majority, will go after those aspects of the fiscal budget that they have selected as their personal wind-mill(s). Administrative and/or teacher salaries will rank high on their hit list. Extracurricular athletic and non-athletic activities will also receive attention. If the teacher's contract is current-ly under negotiations, then class size and health benefits will also be targets for increases and decreases respectively. These are but the classic targets. Depending upon the scope of negativism and disenchantment with the school system as a whole, other areas for scrutiny will emerge, as per the prej-udices of our respective FWDs.

The negative effects upon a school district's mission to provide a competitively qualitative educational environment where each student has the opportunity to become all that he/she can be has long term and destructive consequences for the school system. When Mrs. Rosalyn Carter, the President's well-respected wife and then First Lady, com-mented upon Presidents Reagan's victory in the 1980 elec-tion, she observed that the President-elect's popularity with the voters stemmed in part from the fact that "...he [Reagan] made Americans feel comfortable with their prejudices..." This is the case with our FWDs. They expand upon the dislikes, anger, and prejudices of school district residents and proceed to direct their worst nature's unhappiness towards the so-called frailties of the public schools. High taxes, disobedient children (including their own), perceived absences of author-ity, poor comparative test scores with other districts/ states/nations, and the lack of a proper moral/ethical envi-ronment in which to educate our youth are cleverly utilized by FWDs to focus the public's frustrations upon various aspects of the school district's educational budgetary plan.

The most ethically defective of the FWDs will use their position on the Board as a bully pulpit to whip up antagonism towards, and suspicion of, every action which anyone in the educational community undertakes. Board meetings provide the forum for the FWD to conduct McCarthy-like interrogations of the administrative budget-makers, questioning every item in a given category right down to whether the students' donuts should be frosted or just plain. The meaner of the FWD species is arrogant, argumentative, and ill-mannered. They will consistently misrepresent and/or distort a budgetary line item so as to create the illusion that the so-called educators with all their degrees are not very bright and somewhat incompetent. A favorite ploy of the FWD is to promote oneself as a true representative of the people and describe in detail before an audience inclusive of the media how a multitude of constituents have encouraged the FWD to go for it. In matter a fact he/she received only two or three phone calls from the taxpayers anxious to use our FWD for their own purposes.

The venom of negativism and doubt which the FWD injects into the community results in defeated school budgets and/or critical reductions in the resources, both human and physical, which are vital for the effective delivery of the educational mission. As in the case with the People's Republic of China during the disastrous decade of the Cultural Revolution, 1966-76, it may take years and years of reconstruction for a District to makeup for the disastrous void created by a few misdirected and mischievous egos.

The El Cid

The El Cid or Noble Leader is in almost every facet the direct opposite of the financial watchdog. Those school districts that have a majority of such persons on the Board invariably are the systems that manage to out-perform, ceteris paribus, other school districts on a consistent basis regardless of size or location.

The El Cid(s) are a unique combination of virtue, integrity, and self-effacement. They have made a commitment to the youth of not only their own school system but to youth universally. They are generally motivated by a desire to provide the best education possible to all the students. They operate on the philosophical triad of quality, equity, and progress. They are actually conscious of, as demonstrated in their voting records, the heavy responsibility which the stewardship of an entire school system places upon them.

To a stranger attending a school Board meeting for the first time they are easily recognizable. Their tone of voice is calm and restrained. They listen to other members of the Board before they comment and/or offer rebuttal. They are polite and civil to each other and members of the audience even when such members are themselves less than civil. Also, and this may appear amusing to the reader, they don't appear to be angry or mean-looking. The easiest method of identifying the El Cids is when they sit next to or directly across from the fiscal watchdogs. It is like night and day. The FWD invariably will at some point resemble a pit bull who has not been fed. The FWD invariably snarls, grimaces, pounds the table, sneers at those who disagree with him, hurls both disguised and open insults at them, and, in general, conducts himself in a manner that creates a climate of adversarial confrontation.

Where the FWD is invariably a male, although a few unforgettable females have occupied the role, our El Cid is more evenly distributed in terms of gender. However, over the years it has been the distaff side who has most consistently achieved the high moral and ethical standards alluded to previously. As a teacher, taxpayer, and parent, I more often than not encouraged, worked for, and voted for women to be members of the B.O.E. In almost every instance I was not disappointed by their performance, even when it differed from what I thought it should be. It was always my openly stated wish and objective to have an all-female Board. If such a Utopian ideal were ever realized I reasoned then as a teacher, taxpayer, and parent I could sleep secure at night. Some of you who read this will say it smacks of sexism. But make no mistake about this; the motivation is practical and totally objective. It has been this author's experiences that over the years female B.O.E. members are more open-minded to suggestions whatever the source; are considerably less egotistical than their male counterparts; exhibit less negativism and more positive attitudes towards education; are not lawyers, but are mothers; are more polite and civil to people; and are seldom monolithic in their purpose for being on the Board.

School districts that have had the good fortune to have its residents opt for the El Cid type of majority are those districts that invariably are at or near the top of the statistical charts for student achievement. The nobility of selfless leadership exemplified by this breed of Board member seems to have a trickle-down effect on the masses. The positive attitude and unabashed desire to see kids succeed manifests itself within the public domain with an increased confidence in, and effort to support, the local school system. Budgets and bond issues are regularly passed with little acrimony and debate. Do not make the mistake in concluding that the Road to Wellville is not without its potholes and detours. The difference however between the El Cid-type Board member and the FWD-type Board member is that the forum for compromise and rapprochement is more readily available to heal the slings and arrows of outrageous fortune with the former than with the latter.

The Anti-Unionist

This species of Board member ran for the Board of Education and was elected on the strength in most cases of a single issue—that the teachers' union was the primary cause of the dual anathema of the property owner, namely, increasing budgets and high property taxes. The anti-unionist has appealed to the inherent antipathy of the average taxpayer towards government spending with a carefully designed propaganda program revealing increased teacher salaries, either in excess of equal to the average salary of the district's residents. He/she has been quick to point out the fact that teachers only work approximately 185 days a year which includes a work assignment liberally flavored with an enviable schedule of vacation time. The anti-unionists strategy is protracted labor negotiations. At the time, the anti-unionist will portray the union's teachers as greedy and oblivious to the local taxpayer's fiscal plight. He/she will create a biased statistical picture, using manipulated data which leads to a single, conclusion that the teachers in all fairness should take a pay-freeze for the duration of the new agreement as well as give back certain benefits which have already been won by the union in past agreements.

The temporary malaise and disaffection of the community will be interpreted by our anti-unionist as a mandate to clean-up the union's act, monitor the teachers' professional performance, and insure accountability to the public. For the over-zealous anti-unionist this effort takes on the dimension of a messianic mission to destroy the Philistines and deliver the school district back to its real owners, the beleaguered taxpayer. The strident call to return to the people their independent property rights, i.e., schools, is a manifestation of the anti-unionists general dislike and suspicion of any agency of government and especially one that directly affects the tax rates. Any perceived agent of a government sub-division, i.e. teacher, which represents the threats of increased taxation becomes the enemy. Henceforth, unions that bargain for and represent teachers become woven into our Mme. DeFarge's tapestry to be dealt with at a future time.

The antipathy which our DeFarge anti-unionist harbors has a universal element to it. All unions are bad but confusingly enough teachers are not all bad in the eye of the anti-unionist. Somehow, and it is never made quite clear how, the teachers have been swayed and/or duped by a few persuasive activists into betraying their professed loyalty to the district and transferring it to the union. Therefore, in order to save face and not appear as anti-teacher, the anti-unionist portrays the teachers as victims of an oligarchical conspiracy by the union's leadership to use the politics of confrontation and adversarial relations in order to achieve their own personal agendas. The ignorant anti-unionist actually believes this conspiracy theory and groups teachers into a separate category outside of union membership. The manipulative anti-unionist will attempt to separate the teachers from their union membership utilizing bogus issues such as role models for students, responsibility for educating all students, maintaining a positive public image, budget failure at the polls, and concern for the taxpaying public.

Along with the anti-unionist's perception that any organization representing labor is inherently subversive to the Founding Father's democratic ideals, there exists another personal motivation that feeds the fires of anti-union resentment. The skeleton in the anti-unionist's closet takes the shape of socio-economic status. For if the truth were really known, those individuals who are elected to Boards of Education on an anti-union bias are in fact jealous and/or envious of the gains obtained by teachers' unions over the past three decades. The marked improvement in the terms and conditions affecting the employment status of teachers especially as it concerns salaries and benefits is viewed as an alarming state of affairs to this breed of Board member.

The perception that teachers, under the auspices of their unions, have either reached, are approaching, or exceed the income levels of certain occupations and/or professions is a bothersome if not loathsome condition. This revelation parallels a similar sequence of events within the context of the civil rights and feminist movements. Each of these advancements in human affairs was marked by a relatively swift change in the historic status of minorities, women, and teachers. The comfortable feeling which accompanies conformity to and observance of certain socio-economic norms was suddenly lost. Teachers, a one-time docile and self-effacing cohort, made demands upon Boards of Education and demonstrated in the public forum when those demands were not satisfactorily met. These and subsequent confrontations with school authorities resulted in the emergence of a group of individuals who were motivated in the fashion of Talleyrand after the Napoleonic wars, to turn back the tide of change and return to the former status quo, before the Taylor law.

The Napoleonic model appropriately defines sovereignty as the paramount issue. Each school district in a qualified sense is a sovereign entity with its own rules or laws, hierarchy of authority, and procedural formalities. For almost two centuries school boards and committees both possessed and exercised almost absolute power and authority in regards to the "...superintendence, management, and control of the educational affairs of the district..." And then, as Napoleon had done in Europe, the union movement caught up with the public sector and proceeded to challenge that bastion of absolute power and authority. It was projected that the unions posed, as they continue to do, a dire threat to the Board of Education's power and authority to act independently and preemptively. Therefore, in the eyes of the anti-unionist, it is an obligation and duty to stem the tide of teacher sovereignty and return the schools back to their proper and previous masters, the B.O.E. With their guidance and authority a quality educational program can yet be offered within the confines of a conservative fiscal plan.

The reader should not doubt for a moment that the issue of sovereignty is paramount. It is historically recorded, as with the dichotomy of the Japanese Imperial throne and that of the office of Shogun, that the legitimate repository and exercise of sovereignty does not always reside within the same governing institution. The unions and anti-unionists simultaneously perceived the advent of collective bargaining as the potential vehicle for transferring sovereignty, at least in part, from the Board of Education to the union.

The Politician

This species of Board member views a seat on the B.O.E. as either a stepping stone towards higher public office and/or a vehicle wherein one's socio-political philosophies and prejudices will receive a legitimately recognized forum to be heard. The politician may or may not be supported either openly or clandestinely by a political organization. In either case, the politician will perform as if in fact they were running for or occupied a political office. The politicization of a B.O.E. is perhaps the worst fate that can befall a school district due to the fact that educational priorities eventually become secondary.

In the urban setting the politico Board member is more likely to be connected with an historical political entity, i.e., Republican or Democratic parties. This is not necessarily the case in a suburban setting. There the politicization process will more often than not take the form of a locally organized faction that will either put up candidates who represent their platform or support those Board incumbents who appear sympathetic. When elected to the B.O.E., the politician who either openly or under the guise of a "return to basics" platform will use any and all agenda items to advance a political agenda. No matter how apolitical an issue may be, whether it's class size, textbook selection, plain or sugar donuts for the cafeteria, school colors, or school mascot, our political stalwart will convert it into a "them versus us" confrontation. Unfortunately, in too many instances the original intent of the agenda item or proposal will be lost or placed out of context in order to serve the politician's purpose(s).

If in a minority, the politician's effect may be one of prolonging discussion at best and impugning the motivations and integrity of other non-aligned members at worst. If in a majority, then disaster of Titanic proportions beckons on the horizon as the educational program becomes the pawn to be sacrificed on the political battlefield. The political majority's agenda will be promoted at every B.O.E. meeting with little regard for the niceties of courtesy and respect. The Superintendent of Schools, unless he/she toadies to the majority, may be one of the first victims. In one instance this author believes that it was a key factor in the physical demise of a school Superintendent. The old charge of Lord Acton, that "power corrupts and absolute power corrupts absolutely" is conclusively demonstrated. Insults, insinuations, diatribes, and half-truths become the medium of exchange as one faction after another and advocates of educational reform are swallowed up in a series of confrontations over what would appear as conflicting pedagogical ideologies but what is in fact a struggle for power.

The media, eternally seeking the controversial tidbit in local news, will smell blood and, as vultures to a banquet, immediately begin the autopsy of the proposed corpse. The school district will become an objet de ridicule and controversy within the regional setting. Board meetings will be dissected and analyzed for their entertainment value as well as their attention to educational issues. The local district will be identified as a problem district and held to a microscopic standard of performance unlike other school districts. The loss in prestige, reputation, and self-esteem is immeasurable. The mark of Cain will be branded onto its identity as a district that has to be carefully monitored and watched periodically. Do the Japanese, Taiwanese, South Koreans, or French experience the same gauntlet?

The Pseudo-Intellect or Pontiff

All Boards of Education at one time or another become the habitats of the pontifical Board member. This species, usually limited to the singular in number, is in the prose of the conservative, Thomas Sowell, the "self-anointed paragons of intellectual aptitude." They can be readily recognized at a Board meeting by their sardonic smile and barely tolerant demeanor towards fellow Board members. They are particularly adroit, especially during heated debate over a simple issue, at interjecting with a self-satisfying explanation about the causes, effects, and solutions to the problems. All this of course is accomplished by the utilization of timing and an intimidating vocabulary which leaves most if not all of the remaining Board members either in awe and/or confusion.[5]

For our pseudo-intellectual, each Board meeting and each agenda item affords him the opportunity to pontificate before an audience. No matter how relatively minor a topic may be, this individual is prepared to deliver a papal bull on the subject with a completely complex analysis and/or vocabulary. Though this is intended to clarify, it in fact obfuscates and obscures the issues. The time which is consumed by this person's egotistical gambit is costly both in terms of interpersonal Board relationships and equitable deliberation of all agenda items.

The erudite quality of the pseudo-intellectual's commentary is intended to impose upon his Board colleagues the obvious superiority of his argument and henceforth the necessity of supporting his position by not challenging it. Those who have the temerity to challenge him are greeted with a salvo of five-syllable verbiage more often than not resulting in the hasty retreat of the challenger. However, much to the delight of this writer, there have been moments during heated debate when more daring Board members have requested, much to his chagrin, that our pontiff repeat his verbiage since much of what he had said was untranslatable.

Other stereotypical caricatures exist, but time and inclination do not permit an in-depth exposure but do require mention. Among such prototypes are the Jock Board member whose primary if not sole purpose for being on the Board is to preserve and/or guarantee the existence of the athletic program. Little is ever heard from this individual again once his/her children's sports participation ends or they graduate. There also is an omnipresent representation of the legal profession. By nature this type is conservative, well-dressed (as if for a court appearance), and vociferous on most agenda items. The best ones are strong and consistent advocates for student rights and interests, looking upon them as clients in need of representation. The worst of this genre are ultra-conservative, suspicious of the professional educational community's motivations, and relish the role of the Grand Inquisitor whenever an issue involving professional judgment and/or policy is on the docket.

Last, but certainly not least, is the minimally educated, high school graduate or drop-out whose victory at the polls was based upon a platform of returning the schools back to the people and the basics. You can spot this species quickly. They attend Board meetings generally dressed in work clothes in order to effect an image of the masses, and they take particular relish in demonstrating their ignorance of the English language and/or any other agenda item they don't understand by stating "If it were written/explained in plain English I wouldn't have to ask so many questions!" This type presents as the real, fiscal watchdog, by carefully analyzing and questioning the cost-benefits of plain donuts versus sugared donuts, purchase of used vehicles versus new vehicles, the type of tar used to maintain the district's roofs, and whether money can be saved by making sure that the teachers shut the lights out in their rooms each time they leave them.

In conclusion, let it be stated for the record that any citizen who ventures forth to seek election to a local Board of Education is about to sail upon an ocean whose depth and unrest will consume every moment of their lives. Bon voyage!

Notes

1 . Overton H. Taylor, A History of Economic Thought, (New York: McGraw-Hill Book Co., 1960), 488-492.

2 . Conrad Schirokauer, A Brief History of Chinese and Japanese Civilizations, 2nd ed. (Orlando: Harcourt, Brace, Jovanovich College Publishers, 1989), 442-444.

3 . The World Almanac and Book of Facts: 1999, 373.

4 . Paul M. Angle, ed. The Lincoln Reader, (New Brunswick: Rutgers University Press, 1947), 334-336.

5 . Thomas Sowell, Insider American Education: The Decline, The Deception, The Dogmas, (New York: The Free Press, 1993), 118-119.

Chapter Four

The Administrators

4

The Administrators: Leaders or Laggards?

The United States Marine motto invoking search for a "few good men" could summarize this author's qualitative experience with the administrative division of a school's instructional staff. Over the years it has been a privilege to work with a handful of male/female administrators who I respected and whose friendship I esteemed. But only a handful. The overwhelming majority of this breed were either at, below, or slightly above mediocrity. It appears that the so-called Peter Principle is perhaps more applicable to the education profession than any other since without fail, every superintendent, principal, supervisor, and department chair that I have known has risen up from the teacher ranks. In education it is the nature of the beast.

In most other professions you are educated and trained to be an engineer, lawyer, physician, dentist, pilot, etc. Not so in education. You are educated to be a teacher, not an administrator. In order to be a superintendent or principal you must first serve your time as a teacher. This unique tracking system has been so indelibly imprinted on the profession's learned behavior for so long that it is taken as axiomatic. Interestingly enough, scant research has been devoted to this phenomenon. For example, an individual wishing to be a surgeon goes to a medical school for surgeons. That individual does not have to serve time as an orderly, nurse, nurse's aide, or general practitioner before becoming a surgeon. An airline pilot is not required to serve time as a bagger, ticket seller, or flight attendant in order to qualify for a pilot's license. Likewise, an engineer is not required to serve time as a laborer or foreman in order to become an engineer. Not so in the realm of education.

This author believes that the aforementioned phenomenon is the Achilles Heel in administrative preparation and vocational selection. Instead of holding out the carrot of higher salary and liberation from the tedium of the classroom, schools of education at the collegiate level should initiate, encourage, and provide for an undergraduate degree in administrative arts/science, i.e., a B.A.A. or B.A.S. Such an enterprise would create a fully accredited program which would provide a continuous supply of professionals whose primary vocational career choice is to run a building or a school district and not escape from teaching.

I heartily agree with those readers who would point out that classroom experience is mandatory in order to responsibly conduct the educational mission of a school district. However, any intelligent and rational individual who has attended public school, grades K-12, would be able to satisfy the classroom experience requirement through observation and participation. This author would propose a course of study leading to a bachelor's degree in Administrative Studies, immediately followed by a fifth-year internship in the primary administrative positions within the elementary, middle, and high school. The successful completion of a fifth year would lead to a master's degree in Administrative Studies/Arts, i.e., M.A.S./ M.A.A.

A recommended undergraduate program would, within a general context, approximate the following suggested course of study and application:

Freshman Year

A. *Liberal Arts Survey:*

    1.English structure/usage; literary application/appreciation.

    2.Social Sciences:Western/Easterncivilization/culture;

       Economics;Government.

    3. Math: Statistics; Basic Math; Algebra.

    4. Languages: Survey courses

       in Spanish/French/Russian/Japanese/Chinese (Electives)

B. *Classroom/Building Visitation/Observation: grades*

K-6 within an urban; suburban; rural; private/public school environment

Sophomore Year

A. *Courses of Study*

    1. Guidance/Psychology

    2. Art Appreciation: all aspects of creative/classical art;

       ceramics

    3. Music Appreciation: (Participant and/or observer)

       a. Band

       b. Orchestral

       c. Choral

       d. Western/Eastern

    4. Health/Physical Education

       a. Interscholastic/Intramural

       b. Public Health/Red Cross Life-Saving

       c. Sports Theory/Medicine

5. Science (Elective)
   a. Biology
   b. Chemistry
   c. Physics
   d. Geology
6. Technology
   a. Computer
   b. Audio/Visual

B. *Classroom/Building Visitation and Observation of Middle school (5-8) within an urban; suburban; rural environment*

Junior Year

A. *Courses of Study*

1. Business Economics
   a. Accounting
   b. Math
   c. Statistics
   d. Keyboarding
   e. Computer
2. Administrative
   a. School Management Theory/Practice
      i. District/building-wide
      ii. Subject areas
   b. Public finance and taxation
      i. State
      ii. Local
3. Education Theory/Practice
   a. Classroom/instructional pedagogy
      i. Elementary: Reading/Math
      ii. Middle School: Organization/Goals
      iii. HighSchool:*Planning/Organization/Scheduling*

> b. *Educational Psychology*
>
> c. *Learning models/styles/research*

B. *Classroom/Building Visitation and Observation of high schools (9-12) within an urban, suburban, and rural environment*

Senior Year

A. *Areas of Specialization: Elementary, Middle School, or High School should be selected. Concentration and study within each candidate's area of specialization stressing appropriate:*

1. Subject/course matter
2. Management Styles
3. Budgetary/Financial application
4. Scheduling/Guidance application
5. Labor-Management Relations

B. *Written thesis and/or demonstration regarding a specific education problem in one's area of specialization and proposed solutions and/or resolutions of same.*

Fifth Year

The fifth and final year of preparation would be spent as an intern in an elementary, a middle, and a high school.

This proposed five-year experimental program in Administrative Studies leading to a master's degree in Administration is not written in stone. Some readers may take issue with the subject content and/or organizational plan. It is the author's view that whatever the substance and/or arrangement, the time for a coordinated program in administrative studies is far overdue. It is hoped that some enlightened collegiate administrators and/or chairpersons of Schools of Education will or already are proceeding down this less traveled path.

It is this author's belief that the creation and institutionalization of a career ladder solely for administrative office will go a long way towards providing schools with candidates and educators of the highest professional caliber. Five year renewable contracts, based on performance and leadership criteria which is evaluated periodically, should be implemented. A just cause and/or fair dismissal procedure must accompany the contractual language so that any administrator at any level does not serve at the arbitrary pleasure of a Board of Education majority which may wish to micro-manage a district through the offices of puppet administrators. This author believes that such an arrangement, i.e., limited contractual security and just cause/fair dismissal, would greatly accelerate both the qualitative and quantitative pool of administrative candidates.

Another factor that requires our attention is the gender of the current administrative population. A 1990-91 report by the United States government found that 73 percent of public school teachers were females, with only 33 percent occupying principalships. Even less women occupied the highest office, Superintendent of Schools. Although these statistics are somewhat dated and have improved quantitatively, it is evident that a career ladder for women in administration needs to be reemphasized and advanced further. The primary reason for attention being paid to this uneven gender ratio has less to do with equity than with the potential loss of highly qualified and capable women who could and should be in the administrative ranks.[1]

Despite the fact that a variety of administrative titles prevail within the educational bureaucracy, this chapter will deal primarily with what are viably the three most critical: Superintendent(s), Business Manager(s), and Principal(s). The residuals or wannabes such as assistant principals, athletic directors, district-wide supervisors, and assistant superintendents will be dealt with as space permits since in essence these positions entail functions which obviously are necessary to the system but are either regarded alternatively as terminal sinecures or waiting rooms in terms of the professional ambitions of many of its occupants.

The author does not wish to mislead the reader by implying that such positions are unneeded. It is, however, our intent to focus in on those key positions or people that are most critical to both the day-to-day as well as the long-term management of the school district. The other aforementioned offices are of a secondary importance whose significance is usually in direct proportion to the size of the student population.

We now proceed to investigate the character and make-up of those men and women who have aspired to and achieved at the local school district level the office of what the legal profession considers as an appointment to the bench: the Superintendent of Schools. It is a title and office which was and is intended to strike awe and subservience in its audience whether within the education community or outside it. The legal code in most states enjoins the position with a power and authority which enables it to be one of the few remaining bastions of near absolute power in the United States.

Prior to the advent of pro-active Boards of Education and the concomitant rise of teacher unions, the office was Olympian in terms of its control and authority over the entire gamut of educational decision-making and implementation thereof. It was also Olympian in another manner—its distance from and demeanor towards the school community and the

general community-at-large. As was the case with most institutions and positions of authority in the United States during
the 1960s, the issue of sovereignty, both in terms of residency
and exercise thereof became paramount. Few, if any, offices
or positions of authority were left unscathed by the blistering
challenge to such authority. Although, not a specific target of
this revolution, the Superintendent, as the natural leader of
the so-called public school establishment, came under careful scrutiny. This author believes that the radical changes in
the perception of how America was to be governed at all levels and by whom marks a watershed in the public's newly
conceived view of how and by whom its schools would be
run. A more vital and what has proved to be the premier issue
that evolved from that decade of transformation was the
determination of the definition of the public schools' mission
and purpose.

It was advocated that the public schools would provide
both the vehicle and the panacea for the solution of
America's socio-economic ills. The acceptance of this historic
mandate by the educational community from an aroused
American public made the administration of a school system
an infinitely more complicated affair. Society's problems,
instead of being stopped at the schoolhouse door, were
included as part of its mission. The resulting broadening of the
schools' proffered services radically changed the mission of
our public schools and with it the once carefully defined role
of the Superintendent of Schools.

The increased demands being placed on all members of
the educational community was no more keenly felt than at
the Superintendent's office. A different approach and a different philosophy was required to meet the strident if not
somewhat unrealistic demands of a frustrated public. In

essence, a new type of CEO for our schools became compulsory. The individual who once aspired to be the educational leader by law, must now become the educational leader in practice and by example. A new breed of Superintendent was demanded. The gates of the fiefdom had been breached! A populist ideology, seeking to enfranchise all socio-economic denominations into the ruling order, confronted the District's CEO. The management of the educational institution became ancillary, in some cases, to the management of the community at large. This of course meant that a fairly sophisticated public relations program had to be implemented in order to 'sell' the schools to a once docile constituency that had awakened from its Rip Van Winkle slumber. Parental input which had been limited to Open House festivities in the past, now became frequent, knowledgeable, and critical about the rudiments of pedagogical technique(s) and philosophy. Everyone now knew how the schools should be run!

Perhaps the most armor-piercing even that resulted from the tumult of the Sixties was the emergence of and rise to prominence of public-employee unions. As noted elsewhere in this book the sixties also gave rise and credibility to the women's and civil rights movements. This tripartite challenge to the established authorities in all sectors of American life resulted in a furious reassessment of traditional attitudes and conduct that had been unquestionably accepted. In the realm of formal education the effects were revolutionary. No longer did teachers ask or implore of a condescending, if not openly contemptuous, Board of Education the necessity for remuneration that was in keeping with the responsibility and training that was inherent to the education of America's youth.

For Superintendents of Schools this was an extremely difficult if not traumatic period. The gender and race issues could wait. It was the union issues of recognition and the right to bargain collectively over terms and conditions of employment that became paramount. One can only guess at the number of Superintendents and principals who did not envision the new order as being to their liking and opted for retirement. Coming to terms with teachers at the bargaining table as equals was not within the realm of their perception of the educational order of things.

For those administrators who remained on board and/or were not close enough to retirement there proceeded a period of acclimation. For those relatively new administrators, especially Superintendents, the gauntlet was picked up and the challenge enjoined. For this breed of head administrator the management of a school system would require the skill of a juggler, the wit of Will Rogers, the patience of Job, and the leadership of an F.D.R. Of those Superintendents whom I served with, and they were nine in number, only two approached or met the preceding criteria. The rest were not incompetent but failed in that single criteria so universally required of a CEO, President, Prime Minister or Superintendent—leadership.

To this teacher the key to any relationship between the educational head of the school district and his/her staff was whether the crucial element of mutual respect was evident. In the old days respect came by association with title or position. After the sixties, it had to be earned. In my career this element was always the key in determining the basis of my relationship as a teacher and grievance chairperson with any administrator, especially the Superintendent of Schools. I did not have to like him/her, just respect their content of character and ability to lead. The mutual component of that respect was what generally broke down in the professional relationship process. Since I wore two hats, teacher and grievance chair, most of the administrators in our school district saw only the latter. With the exception of two superintendents and one principal I was the annual recipient of the Preparation-H Award, for being the biggest pain in the ass to administrators.

To those three administrators who I worked with, my image was not perceived as threatening or a challenge to their authority. I believe, although the subject was never broached with any of the three, that they viewed an individual such as myself as a colleague whose performance and integrity as a union leader was to be evaluated on the same basis as my integrity and performance as a classroom teacher. Despite the difference in statutorial authority I can never recall being treated as anything but an equal by these people. Our mutual respect for one another and practiced willingness to share decision-making created a positive and educationally invigorating environment which permeated the entire instructional staff. I was never reluctant to share with my teaching colleagues the fact that any gains and/or improvements in their terms/conditions of employment would not have been possible without the mutual respect and cooperation of those administrators.

What a contrast this was to that of most of the other administrators whose perception of me was akin to that of a Mephistopheles or Svengali. To them, a person such as myself represented a threat to their authority and power. In their limited perception, the union constituted a sinister force bent upon usurping the power and authority of those individuals who by law were entrusted to possess and exercise it. This observation may appear somewhat grandiose in its dimensions, but the reader should not doubt for a moment that the anti-union bias which has historically existed in our nation, was indeed present within the educational bureaucracy's higher echelons. Let it be stated for the record that those Superintendents who were most guarded and conscious of their authority recorded the most grievances and prolonged collective bargaining confrontations during their tenures. Similarly, those administrators who exercised their authority in imperial fashion had their buildings visited by the grievance chair most frequently. Enough said.

At this juncture some commentary is required about an office and individual whose importance to the school district as a whole is second only to that of the Superintendent of Schools—the Assistant Superintendent for Business, or Business Manager. There are some who are of the opinion that this person is the de facto top banana in the school district. Similar in many respects to the Chairman of the Federal Reserve System, the fiscal acumen and monetary talents of this person can without contravention make or break a school system's educational mission and future development. In many school systems the Business Manager is a bit of a mystery person, coming into full light between February and June. During this period of time that most feared and simultaneously worshiped icon of all school systems, the budget, is developed, fashioned, debated, altered, and finally submitted to the district's residents for approval.

We must pause at this time to introduce the uninitiated into that vast complex of laws, regulations, and practices which compromise the somewhat mysterious underworld of public school finance and funding. Far from being expert in such matters, but having an informed layman's knowledge of same, this writer will attempt to layout the big picture of public school finance. Even to those readers who have been exposed to public finance academically and/or career-wise, public school finance represents a whole new ball game.

As an illustration of the unique qualities which set public school finance apart from all other financial/budgetary systems, I am reminded of an incident which occurred in a school district a number of years ago. It seems that during a period of discontent and contrived disillusionment with the budgetary process and property tax levies, a group of irate taxpayers organized themselves into a Taxpayers Association. Needless to say, they carefully orchestrated a campaign to convince the voters that continued budgetary excesses resulting in high taxes were being foisted onto the district's residents by a school administration intimidated by a powerful local teacher's union. They handily won the election and quickly set a course to reform the budgetary process and control the fiscal pocketbook. As part of their design they installed a retired finances and budgetary specialist from a well-known industrial corporation to chair the local budget advisory committee. It would be his job to apply hard-bitten and classic private-sector financial strategies which would eliminate the waste and fat in the budget. Misled by his friends in the new Board of Education majority, this gentleman was quickly and painfully introduced to the world of public school finance at the first meeting of the lay budget advisory committee. His knowledge of private sector finances had not prepared him for the nuances of public school finance. It is to his credit that he made the conversion from mentor to student expeditiously.

It was the Assistant Superintendent for Business or Business Manager for the school district who in his role as advisor to this committee, became the mentor. He had an apt pupil, who speedily adapted to another world of budgetary finance, i.e., public school finance. The relatively uncomplicated financial universe of the private sector gave way to the complexities of factors such as state aid ratios; multi-faceted taxing units, i.e., towns/villages; and mandated state programs and contingency budget voting to name a few. I recall the new chair of the committee referring to the public school finance system's intricacies as mind-boggling. Needless to say, many of the misconceptions and the perceptions which had been carefully prepared for the new chair of the lay budget advisory committee were cleared up and an appreciation, if not admiration, for the effort needed to compile data and prepare a budget which would affect the lives of thousands of students was instilled.

The principle purpose for describing the preceding scenario in such detail was to introduce to the reader the real power behind the throne, the 'money-man' or Business Manager. In my experience the individual who has occupied what I consider to be the most critical administrative position in the school system has been a low-profile number cruncher whose business acumen and knowledge of education finance law and its application determine the quantity and quality of the school district's educational program. In most school districts with a K-12 population ranging from 2,500 to 7,000 students, the Business Manager will earn between $65,000 and $85,000 annually, depending upon experience. These figures are generally 15 to 20 percent lower than the Superintendent of Schools' salary, all other things being equal. Obviously the two positions are not comparable in respect to duties and authority as defined by statute and practice. However, if one compares the two positions in terms of value to the entire school system a strong argument can be made to equalize the two salaries.

At present, the New York Superintendents of Schools' powers/duties are governed by section 1711 of the Education Law, the New York State Rules and Regulations of the Commissioner of Education, case law as determined by the judiciary, and other applicable statutory enactments regarding teachers and students. Much of the Superintendent's duties are public relations oriented, with his/her primary constituents being the public and the local Board of Education. Contact and communication with teachers and students is generally delegated to other administrative staff members. Satisfying, informing, and an over-all cultivation of the Board of Education heads the Superintendent's list of priorities.

The most honored and revered method of keeping the Board happy is for the Superintendent to prepare (enter the Business Manager) and present a school budget which will include minimal annual percentage increases with a concomitant minimal impact on the local property tax rate. If such action can be performed consistently on an annual basis in association with an ongoing public relations program which promotes and maximizes the successes of the school system while placating and/or stroking those community elements which could cause trouble then all is well in Mudville. The last factor on the Superintendent's list of priorities is akin to that of a celebrity, namely, to make appearances at meetings both within and outside the school community, and make presentations at various school-related functions.

There still remains an aura, although somewhat diminished, surrounding the title of Superintendent of Schools. The possession of the title must create a harmony of illusion that he/she also possesses the wisdom, knowledge and intellect which the lay community assumes is inherent in the holder of such appellation. An enlightened individual who occupies this office should know Education Law, keep abreast of case law, and know the local labor contracts, especially the teachers'. Most of the general lay community is almost totally ignorant of the laws, rules, regulations, and procedures governing the operation and direction of a school district. The shrewd Superintendent of Schools armed with this knowledge will be successful at maintaining the required aura of intellectual superiority cloaked within a carefully scripted image of respected mentor to the masses.

The third player in our administrative trilogy provides the real foundation for the administrative leadership function within any school district. In concert with the instructional staff, the principal of a building makes or breaks the successful delivery of a school building's educational mission. He/she is the line officer on the battlefield of public school education. The principal is in the trenches with his/her troops, i.e., teachers, encouraging and motivating them to implement tactics and strategies which will destroy the enemies—ignorance, indifference, and apathy.

As is the case with all administrators, the principal has served time in the classroom previous to serving as principal. Reasons for leaving the classroom are not complicated or vague. In the past, i.e., before the 1960s, the vast majority of aspiring administrators viewed the office of principal as the primary and final resting place for their administrative ambitions. It was not that such individuals were averse to rising through the ranks either by retirements or deaths. It was more a matter of monetary consideration in association with limited ambition. This was especially the case for men in the elementary tenure area where the monetary status and prestige of the principalship, was the vehicle by which they could escape the ignominy of being one of two males on the faculty surrounded by hordes of prepubescent youngsters. There was an unspoken but generally accepted perception shared especially by the general public and somewhat within the teaching profession that questioned the virility of a man who made a career of teaching third or fourth graders. But then again, there was also a concomitant perception mentioned previously in this text which at one time questioned the virility of any male in American culture who entered a profession dominated by females.

For those individuals of a more ambitious bent, the principalship was the critical stop-over which would determine whether a broader district-wide position of authority and responsibility was to be in their future. Any aspiring Superintendent of Schools had to have, as one does today, tenure in a principalship before advancing on to more Olympian heights. Whatever the ambitions of a principal may be, make no doubt about it that one must make it in this office in order to remain a credible force in the dynamics of any school district's administrative promotional ladder.

In the post-1960s, the demands by parents, teachers, students, and the community at large meant the creation of a position, especially at the middle and high school levels, that requires of its occupant the talent and capacity to perform feats usually accorded to the man from Galilee. Practically speaking, those principals who have functioned most effectively in my experience possessed the following traits and/or skills:

1. The ability to carry their title lightly on their shoulders. By this we mean the ability to perform competently as a principal without constantly reminding the staff and/or students that he/she was the principal.

2. The knowledge of what is going on within the entire building or a reason-

able facsimile thereof. The principal must be attuned to both the staff and student grapevine, especially the latter.

3. The ability to cultivate and hold the confidence and trust of the instructional staff. This obviously is no easy task, given the sensitivities of the staff as promoted by the advent of public unions. It is here that they earn their money, balancing the competing interests of contending departments and factions within the faculty vis-à-vis the growth and development of the educational program as they envision. It is incumbent upon principals to articulate their educational plan(s) in such a manner that the instructional staff perceives itself to be an active participant and advisor whose suggestions/ recommendations will be honestly considered, if not implemented.

4. As with the Superintendent of Schools, the chief building administrator must develop and cultivate in a collegial manner a mutually respectful working relationship with the union leadership. This factor cannot be over-emphasized. Regular meetings and an open-door policy between both parties must be implemented within an environment of real mutual respect and an attitude of compromise/cooperation.

5. Visibility. The principal must be seen as frequently as the demands of the job permit. Both students and faculty must observe the performance of his/her duties. The illusion, at least, of daily involvement must be created and maintained. The principal cannot function effectively if he/she is only a voice on the intercom and/or the presenter of awards and suspensions.

6. The principal must create and maintain a presence which defines his/her role and performance in a consistent and positive manner. To the instructional staff he/she must present a knowledgeable and intellectually honest image as one who understands and can be relied upon to critique their progress and his own in a fair and equitable fashion. To the students he must be apart from them but reachable. He cannot be their pal. He/she must make the student body feel comfortable seeing and talking to him. He/she, within the demographic limitations allowed, must create a guru or sensei-like style which allows students to feel that he/she really cares and enjoys being with them.

I cannot resist at this point in calling the reader's attention to that principalship which is the closest to a sinecure, that of elementary principal. No administrative position of authority is unexacting in education, but the elementary principalship comes closest. An elementary school is basically a turn-key operation as far as the head administrator is concerned. His/her primary concerns are keeping his/her staff happy, touring the hallways and grounds, appearing as a mother or father figure to both children and staff alike, and generally looking for something to do. Doing nothing but doing it well can be a job in itself.

What follows next is a series of composite profiles of administrative styles, personalities, and images which the author has experienced and/or observed over the years. Our commentary will be limited to the Superintendency and those individuals who through their performance have either elevated or diminished this august office.

The Invisible Man

This individual has achieved his dream of occupying the highest pinnacle of educational authority. In some respects he likens his title to that of Supreme Court Justice of the United States. He dotes on his authority and protects it jealously, believing that the less contact and communication he has with subordinate staff, students, community, and associates, the safer and more enhanced will be any manifestation of power which he exerts. He perceives his position as well-earned and deserving of his talents. Any question placed to him of a pedagogical nature and/or meeting requested to discuss the same is perceived as a potential threat to his identification as titular educational leader of the district.

This individual is a careful cultivator of the Board of

Education and will toady to their wishes, desires, and/or demands without any real show of leadership while convincing the Board that their ideas/philosophies are very much identical to his own. In order to preserve his job and comfortable income, he will allow the president of the Board and/or certain members of that body to not only make policy but to direct and implement it as well. Maintenance of the status quo is his credo. Anything that suggests a change immediately raises a red flag in regards to his security. The school district ship will remain basically at anchor with all precautions being taken by its captain to avoid the stormy seas of controversy or alteration of the status quo.

This type of Superintendent perceives his position as an end in itself and not as a means to lead his district towards growth and development. He exists only because a Board of Education allows him to exist. He is the most dangerous prototype of educational leadership that a district can have because the preservation of his sinecure, his position, is the primary consideration in any action or inaction that he proposes to undertake. I don't recall whether I read it or heard it from a disconsolate colleague, but there is an axiom that states, "Most Superintendents walk around with a broom attached to their backside, in order to cover their tracks..." If so, our invisible man certainly qualifies as a classical example of broommanship.

The Pontiff

This individual is one of the most fascinating of the Superintendent prototypes. This individual carries his title quite heavily on his shoulders. There is not a waking moment that he is not aware of the title Superintendent of Schools and ownership of same. It is a role that is relished and never is stepped out of. As the Holy Pontiff in Rome is historically responsible for his flock and on religious issues is considered to be infallible in his decisions and pronouncements, so too is our educational pontiff. He considers himself the unchallenged leader of the educational community and therefore expects obedience and loyalty to his judgments and directives. He will generally have an earned doctorate in education (Ed.D.) especially in the urban/suburban school districts. These additional initials after his name in conjunction with his title lends increased legitimacy to his self-endowed claim as the undisputed head of the educational community.

The pontiff's communications will read like papal bulls whether they are directed towards staff or the community at large. He will, as the invisible man prototype, consider any interpretive questions of his pronouncements to be an immediate threat to his authority and position. The local teachers' union and at times the Board of Education will be the primary source of heresy, for it is these two entities that will more times than not pose a threat to the pontiff's suzerainty.

The teacher's union is of course the greatest heretic because the teacher's contract is considered in the same light as Martin Luther's 95 Theses were by the Catholic church. It is the enemy! Any proposals, offers, overtures, and/or requests made by this unholy host must be rejected or denied outright. The pontiff perceives that the ultimate goal of the union is to undermine and subvert his power and majesty. This script obviously results in a relationship of adversarial confrontation between the union and the Superintendent on any issue. The pontiff will look to his college of Cardinals—the Board of Education—for reaffirmation and support, portraying the union as infidels threatening the very fabric of the governance and prerogatives of the Superintendent and Board of Education's established authority.

The depiction of the preceding scenario holds dire consequences for any school district. Both the union and the Superintendent expend unnecessary energy and resources in protecting their respective turfs at the cost of mutually cooperative effort aimed at enhancing the learning environment for the district's students.

Lord of the Manor: The Burden of Title

As with all of our stereotypical archetypes, there are bits and pieces of each profile within every other administrative profile. Therefore, the Lord of the Manor will incorporate certain characteristics more familiar to the pontiff model. What truly distinguishes the Lord-like Superintendent from any other so-called prototype is a preoccupation with the title Superintendent of Schools. It is the raison d'être as the French so succinctly put it, their purpose for existence. The title is carried in Christ-like fashion as one wends his way along the educational Via Dolorosa of life. The title as with the cross is the symbol of the majesty and power of the Lord or Laird. It cannot be put down. The title becomes an almost religious manifestation of sorts with its owner basking in the self-righteous knowledge that the divine-right theory of kingship has found its historic transmutation in the office of Superintendent of Schools.

Twenty-four hours a day, 365 days a year the burden and authority of title are borne. The occupant of the office revels in the sound of the title. As with the Hindu "OM," it becomes a mantra of almost supernatural significance. As an example, our Laird rises in the morning not looking at an individual, but at a title. He subconsciously refers to himself in his private thoughts in titular fashion. Upon arrival at his office he quietly delights in viewing his title and name on the brass plate above his door where once again his need for reaffirmation is reinforced simultaneously with its proclamation about the owner's sovereign authority.

Like Moses' God, he is a jealous Laird and will tolerate no other rival or perceived challenge to his omnipotence. Woe to the secretary, assistant superintendent (whose use of the title is a constant annoyance), or any other individual whom he suspects of usurping the authority of his office. This of course is especially true of the local teacher's union which he perceives in pontiff-like fashion to be a manifestation of the devil. Almost all the union's leadership are looked upon with suspicion and distrust. They are viewed from within the same prism as a subtle or overt attempt to diminish the office and, henceforth, title of Superintendent of Schools. "Off with their heads!" As a final observation, it has been this author's experience that an inverse relationship appears to exist between the physical height of the occupant of the Dragon Throne and its owner's consciousness about his title. Amen.

The Man for All Seasons

Once again in paraphrasing William Faulkner's observation, relating to how a few good teachers can make "all the difference," it was this author's good fortune to work with, not under, two superintendents who made all the difference. As I reflect upon those qualities which evoked my respect and admiration for these two gentlemen, words such as integrity, honesty, forthrightness, courage, independence, and fairness come to mind. Both men were ambitious. Each in his own way sought that career niche in education which would satisfy the itch that each had to scratch. However, in pursuing their own aspirations, they never lost sight of their responsibility and obligation to the local district they were hired to lead. Leadership was the key. They were not afraid to lead and risk antagonizing Board of Education members, community members, and union leaders who were capable of making trouble for them. They weren't afraid of a fight over principles but were always ready to listen and, if necessary, back off if their opponent presented a sounder and more logical argument.[2]

If there was one common denominator which these men for all seasons shared it was their ability to carry their titles lightly. Both held doctorates but preferred honestly to be called by their first names. To this teacher, it meant that I could stand before them as an equal in pursuit of a common goal. As a union negotiator and grievance chairman I had the opportunity if not the advantage of dealing with both men from a confrontational as well as a conciliatory standpoint. No matter how difficult the issue or passionate the emotions, we parted not as enemies but as mutually respected combatants. There were numerous instances when neither the union nor the superintendent could make the necessary compromises in order to reach agreement on a certain issue or issues. This did not stop either party from reaching accord on other matters with a handshake and/or oral commitment. And they always kept their promises (to me, anyway).

As with Sir Thomas More, for whom the movie "A Man for All Seasons" was the subject, so too it is with these Superintendents. They were men of principle whom all could rely on to serve as a model to emulate. When you were in their presence you felt as if they knew you and genuinely cared to hear what you had to say. They knew all of the staff by name, including teachers, secretaries, janitors, bus drivers, and further could talk informally with any of them as if they wore the same hat. This was in stark contrast to one Superintendent whose recognition of the staff was not only marginal but was easily confused between two veteran teachers whose names, Gerry and Gary, sounded alike. After saying hello to this gentleman the conversation rapidly deteriorated and almost instantly was broken off by the mutual discomfort of both parties.

It is this author's unflagging belief that the breed of men for all seasons is rapidly drying up. All school districts historically possess a few. My experience was hopefully not unique. The problem is that the few are becoming fewer! Too many external as well as internal forces and constituencies are making the job nearly impossible. The potential for both men and women for all seasons to appear and lead has become diminished because of the readiness and capacity of Boards of Education, ethnic and racial antagonism, limited public funding, taxpayer revolts, religious zealots, unions, and a pessimistic public to undermine and destroy the ability of the man or woman for all seasons to function, if not exist.

What this leaves us with at the helm of course is the pontiff, the invisible man and the laird of the manor. The pool of top-notch administrators is shrinking. Where the once-upon-a-time 100-150 applicants vied for a superintendency, today that number is generally halved. In the big city arena the life expectancy of a Superintendent, depending on the aggressiveness of the various interest groups on the Board of Education, is in the single digits with five years being a good estimate. These jobs are killers. They are taken by men and women who, like Shakespeare's Cassius, have a "...lean and hungry look." Unlike the literary Cassius, however, who delivers one of the fatal blows to Caesar, it is our Superintendent who is on the receiving end of the "...slings and arrows of outrageous fortune," from Boards of Education and community interest groups. Such Superintendents of Schools have little time or energy to pursue educational innovation and goals to their conclusion. They are too busy surviving in the present and preparing for the next onslaught or attack that is coming.

Superintendents can be compared in some degree to big-time college and NFL coaches. Both are paid well to manage a team of skilled personnel whose goal is to have a winning season followed by a post-season recognition for outstanding performance, i.e., fan support, strong season ticket sales to fans, and budget approval by the voters. Both individuals move around a lot in search of that elusive of all Pimpernels, the perfect environment or setting in which they have all the ingredients for a successful tenure and the recognition by their respective constituencies—fans and community—of their unique capabilities. Most are like the Bedouins of the desert moving from oasis to oasis in search of heaven's eternal water, cool breezes, and shade. Though this may seem too imaginative, this author's personal experience has witnessed this symbiotic relationship more often than not.

When I was in graduate school, in one of those inane but required education courses, I recall a conversation which took place with other inmates who were pursuing degrees and careers in administration. The subject of the conversation turned to the various types of school districts which were deemed to be the most attractive. One of the conversants who was near the end of the academic quest for his administrative credentials made the following pronouncement, "I'm looking for a nice, relatively small district whose student population has stabilized, has no building program in existence or planned for the foreseeable future, and whose voters are in the upper middle class of income earners." The other aspirants nodded their approval, with one of them adding, "A winning football team would be nice, too." This was back in the seventies. Has Utopia changed? I'm not sure.

Notes

1. New York State School Boards Association, School Law, (Albany: New York State School Boards Association, Inc., 1998), 132.

2. William Faulkner, New Orleans Sketches, Carvel Collins, ed., (New York: Random House, 1958), 2.

Chapter Five

The Kids

5

The Kids: Mandarins and Reluctant Scholars

Whenever I heard a comment from fellow colleagues complaining about those damn kids I was always quick to remind them as well as myself that without them we would be unemployed. After four decades of teaching and observing the American student in an urban, suburban, and semi-rural environment it is without reservation that I can say that the experience was both exhausting and exasperating. During this sojourn the author was afforded the opportunity to witness the metamorphosis of the American student at the secondary level in grades 7-12. A brief but sustained pedagogical encounter in the classroom with secondary students in Japan, as well as in India and China in the 1970s and '80s, led me to the conclusion that the American student is one of, if not, the most difficult individuals in the world to teach. The metamorphosis experienced by the author pertains primarily to the changes in attitude exhibited by students over the years in terms of their conception of school and the necessary effort required to succeed within its environs.

The key operative word was and is: attitude. It is the common denominator among all students in the world in terms of effort and achievement in a formal classroom setting. It is the one educational factor that has changed the most since

1960. Attitude decisively affects learning capacity, academic achievement, attendance, and discipline. This observation is not a regional one, for it is the principle characteristic of American secondary students that foreigners immediately become conscious of when exposed to our public schools. Any discussion involving a people's historic attitude towards any subject or topic such as education must by necessity involve cultural bias. Although teachers and schools never truly enjoyed an elevated socio-economic status in our nation's history, they nevertheless were accorded a qualified position of authority and respect. This was due in large measure to society's recognition that the raw material, students, which school authorities received and were responsible for converting into a finished product were capable of testing on a daily basis the patience, skill, and ardor of even the most devoted educational practitioner.

A decision to create compulsory, free public education for the masses is one of the most decisive and risky acts that a nation-state can make in its history. Its purpose in doing so must be clear, consistent, and enforceable in order to guarantee both the perpetuation of the State and the ideals which it postulates. In a closed and/or authoritarian society, admission to and participation in the formal educational experience can be limited to a select class for the express purpose of perpetuating their authority and control over the masses. Ignorance is their most effective control mechanism. In such circumstances the currency of education is highly valued due to its scarcity and close association with exalted socio-economic status. The decision by the State, or nation, to make the once privileged institution of formal education accessible to the masses must be in concert with clear and consistent national objectives.

The case of Japan at the outset of the Meiji Era (1868-1912) is a classic example. Faced with the threat of Western imperialist ambitions and a feudalistically outdated political system, the samurai ruling class of Japan, moved swiftly to create the appearance of modernization, i.e., westernization, in order to preserve their sovereignty. As part of a carefully orchestrated plan to simultaneously delay the Western onslaught which had already reduced China to a quasi-colonial state, as well as catch up to Western technological supremacy, an Imperial Edict on Education was promulgated in 1871. Its purpose was to reinforce Confucian appreciation for the educational process while producing an educated populace devoted, obedient, and loyal to the Imperial polity of Kokutai, a national ethos.[1]

Borrowing from the American system of compulsory school attendance for all children, the Japanese leadership fashioned a national education institution which would provide the new Japan with an educated and competent citizenry capable of meeting if not surpassing the challenge of the West. The reader will in all probability react to the preceding commentary by wryly observing that the then Japanese educational system which was to indoctrinate future generations into unquestioning loyalty to the Imperial throne would eventually lead to a disaster on August 6, 1945. However, a word of caution is in order before a rush to judgment is made. The Japanese did manage both ante-bellum and post-bellum to install an educational work ethic which would compete with the West and withstand the ravages of defeat. The 19th century work ethic which was nurtured and refined by the educational and political bureaucracy continues in full-force today. It is the guiding principle of Japan's educational philosophy.[2]

Each student in Japan is expected to expend the utmost effort in pursuit of academic excellence upon entering the formal classroom experience in the primary grades until graduation from upper secondary or high school. There are no exceptions, save the mentally and/or physically impaired. The standards for achievement are national in scope, not fractionalized and regionalized as in the United States. Autonomy at the local level in Japan has been sacrificed for excellence on a national scale, with the central government, through the Ministry of Education, providing the pedagogical and financial foundation for the entire nation. This organizational and financial framework provides a homogeneous blueprint for successful educational achievement. Such a program however can only be achieved through a national consensus. The United States at this time has no national consensus to adopt such a plan. What we do have is a weak national rhetoric for the adoption of a universal national educational agenda and a lack of the intestinal fortitude to actually enact one.[3]

The effect that the decentralized American educational system has upon student achievement is incalculable. Suffice it to say that there is an inherent disadvantage to a system that encompasses fifty autonomous state-wide educational entities which are further subdivided into many hundreds of quasi-autonomous local municipalities. In such an environment comparative domestic student achievement becomes at best a study in relativity, with each of the myriad sub-units defending their respective turf from federal infiltration by the mantric recitation of their uniquely historical character.

When an American student competes against Japanese, Taiwanese, or South Korean counterparts in international competition, there is an inherent disadvantage due to the mongrel educational preparation that is varied by regional/sub-regional requirements, ethnic/racial discrepancies, and lack of national standards, curriculum, and evaluation instruments. It is truly amazing that American students do as well as they do in these so-called international competitions. The silent factor, which affects any comparative analysis of American students with their international peers, is the historically cherished element known as local control. This characteristic of American education perhaps more so than any other accounts for the disparity in scores and disadvantage which affects the American students performance. For example, let us review the Nebraska state model. It will be utilized not to embarrass its citizenry or vilify its schools but to serve as a profile for measuring the American educational/philosophical framework.

In 1994, Nebraska had approximately 1.6 million residents, with almost 300,000 of them residing in Omaha. The remainder were spread over 535 municipalities in 93 counties and served by no less than 660 school districts. Ten of the nation's least populous counties are in Nebraska, with one of the ten having at last count just 93 citizens. Approximately 350 school districts consist of one elementary school, while 391 districts had a total enrollment of fewer than 200 students. There were 80 one-teacher schools, with some having enrollments of as little as four students! In comparison, New York has 62 counties, a population of 18.1 million, but only 51 more school districts.[4]

The degree of local control existing in Nebraska in concert with a paucity of state-wide standards, curricular controls, and assessment places the students in a precarious position vis-à-vis their efforts in international competition. The uneven and uncoordinated approach within a single state such as Nebraska is mirrored in varying degrees in the other forty-nine. The lack of mandatory curriculum and assessment standards throughout most of the nation in association with the absence of the implementation of a national plan results in an uneven playing field at best. Lower relative test scores are the outcome. This is due in large measure to an educational system which prides itself on local autonomy, evaluative standards ranging from zero to 100 percent, financing based on a regressive property tax structure, and the unrealistic expectation of its constituents attaining world leadership in academic achievement.

A radical shift in national attitudes is required if our children's attitude toward obtaining an education is to incorporate those ideals encompassed within a revived national work ethic which rewards individual instead of ethnic/racial differences, socio-economic status, and genetic aptitude. Students at all levels of schooling are universally sensitive to a common denominator of academic proficiency—expectations. We parents, teachers, and school boards must as with Dickens's hero Pip, convey without qualification society's great expectations of its youth. Our kids will already sense what is expected of them. They too often do not see or perceive a consistent or equitably applied system of expectations. What they do see is a prism of expectations within a crucible of mouthed rhetoric which preaches but seldom delivers a unity of purpose. How many readers recall when the minimum passing grade was 75? Why was it lowered to the national level of 65 or 55? What is the difference in terms of real comprehension between an individual who has failed to grasp 25 percent of a subject's content and one who has been unsuccessful in 35 percent of the same subject content? Was this the beginning of America's sequel to Dickens's Great Expectations—Limited Expectations? Perhaps.[5]

Another issue which has bedeviled educators for at least

the past four decades and one which students are acutely aware of is ability grouping. The classifications are not complex. They consist of two principle models—heterogeneous and homogeneous. The simplicity of the issue however ends there. The philosophical foundations which support each of these organizational models have themselves undergone a metamorphosis of sorts. At the risk of insulting the intelligence of the reader, the author feels compelled to express the fundamental boundaries that delineate these two quintessential models.

The basic premise of homogeneously grouped classes is that if the presentation of material, quality of the material, and the evaluative instruments utilized in measuring student achievement are geared to the student's so-called measured ability level, then each student should hypothetically achieve success: a passing grade. Conversely, the fundamental premise underlying the heterogeneous model is that regardless of ability levels, students placed in such a class structure are expected to meet a specific level of achievement. When all the rhetoric regarding pupil expectations and achievements is reduced to its lowest common denominator, it is how effectively classroom time is utilized that determines the extent of any successful educational outcome.

This issue of classroom grouping of students has in recent years become enmeshed within the national debate regarding standards. The raising of standards for all students regardless of ability levels, with certain qualifications for disabled youngsters, is the educational establishment's designer reform of the moment. Although the goal of raising academic standards in order to compete effectively on an international basis is laudable, the pedagogical methodology of achieving the same remains a dilemma. It is at this juncture that the homogeneous (ability) element and the heterogeneous (single standard based on effort) factor becomes critical to the achievement of the goal sought.

There is no paucity of research studies on this issue. The decision to adopt one method or the other unfortunately becomes embroiled within a socio-economic controversy about race/gender that currently exists within our society. In a nation such as ours, composed of a mosaic of ethnic and racial components competing with and against each other, the aim of achieving higher academic standards provides a welcome forum for a variety of self-interest groups. For instance, to ethnic/racial minorities the standards debate focuses on the question of equal opportunity. African and Hispanic-Americans who all too often occupy the lower rungs of the socio-economic ladder look to an educational system which will guarantee quality and be the ultimate vehicle for escape from the bottom. To them, all students should be grouped together, heterogeneously, with the expectation of meeting the demands of a higher standardized curriculum. The problem however, is that current attitudes and achievement levels among these minorities do not measure up to the expectations which they supposedly endorse.

At present, although modest gains have been achieved in recent years, SAT and reading and math scores, student minorities exclusive of Asian-Americans, rank in the lowest percentiles of academic achievement. How effectively would these students be able to achieve academic success within the context of an educational environment wherein all students are expected to meet higher academic standards successfully? The failure rate would be horrendous. The solution of course would be to revert to a homogeneously organized curriculum wherein special programs based on ability norms could be implemented to raise the skills and competencies of the students until they were ready to reenter the heterogeneous world of monolithic standards. We now have come full-circle and find ourselves once again faced with the continuing dilemma of how to effectively organize the classroom for optimum results. Homogeneous versus heterogeneous, or both?

To further exacerbate the problem we turn our attention to another class of students and their parents who also advocate higher academic standards. For those students who are currently achieving at or above standards—considered by educational authorities as being above the 90th percentile of academic achievement—the preferred pedagogical grouping pattern is homogeneity. Surprise? Not really. Those individuals and/or interest groups who advocate the grouping of students in accordance with the homogeneity of their respective ability level do so in order to preserve and protect the quality of the educational system from a perceived further deterioration. In order to do this, the argument goes, the classroom organizational pattern must be based upon ability and aptitude so that high achieving students are not penalized or punished for their academic success by being condemned to a heterogeneous environment wherein a ceiling is placed on their natural progress. Therefore, many of the homogeneous advocates of the increase in standards movement are motivated in their endorsement by a desire to guarantee the continued success of the nation's most capable academicians while sheltering them from the corrupting influence of those less able and motivated.

Therein, as Shakespeare so aptly put it, "...lies the rub." All parties agree to the proposition of increased academic achievement standards. It is not the end sought but the

means to achieve it that is the devil in the detail. The continuing philosophy of educating young people in our country in
accordance with their so-called ability level and individual
needs is a recipe for the institutionalization of mediocrity. We
are proudly a mongrel nation composed of every ethnic, religious, racial, and philosophical persuasion that exists. The
most powerful, single unifying thread which has kept the fabric of our republic intact is the belief by its citizens that equality of opportunity and success is effectively within the reach of
every American citizen.

The perception of equality of opportunity is always
greater than its reality. Unfortunately, that perception has
dimmed today in the eyes of many Americans who occupy
the lower socio-economic strata of our society. The national
resolve to institute elevated standards and requirements for
high school graduation is based primarily on the discerned
inadequacy of the American student to attain achievement
levels competitive with international peers. I will not go into
the numerous mitigating factors of racial, ethnic, religious, historical, linguistic, and demographic variances which make
such comparisons hazardous if not impossible. I will, however,
in order to illustrate the point, use the Pacific Rim nations as an
example of why international comparisons of academic
achievement can too often be misleading and misplaced.
The people of the Pacific Rim nations generally do not originate or conduct their domestic affairs within the context of a
hybrid society. They basically are homogeneous culturally,
ethnically, and in some cases racially. These people do not
formally recognize, or implement a pedagogical philosophy
wherein the individual needs or abilities of their children are
paramount. Instead, their universally celebrated educational
systems are predicated upon the philosophical foundation

that sustained individual effort will result in a collective high national level of achievement.

Students in South Korea, Taiwan, Singapore and Japan, ability levels notwithstanding, are expected to expend the energy and effort necessary for academic success. Their respective national attitudes of personal pride in accomplishment based upon an unqualified collective effort create the recipe for superior academic achievement.

If, indeed, our schools are to graduate students who are to be proficient enough to compete internationally then we must, as a nation, not raise standards at the outset, but rather escalate markedly the current expectations of our youth's work effort and pursuit of excellence. We must develop and sustain an attitude in our schools that nothing less than an A or 100 is acceptable as a goal! All students must be expected to make the necessary effort in order to achieve this objective. Furthermore, this collective effort is to take place in all subjects, grade levels, and age groups. Until the focus of our pedagogical objectives are focused on attitude and effort instead of individual differences, our continued mediocre educational performance and achievement levels will be maintained.

In recent years the issue of gender recognition as a factor in the learning experience has become a cause celebre. The continuing endeavor by women to obtain equity of opportunity and fair compensation and recognition for their efforts in the workplace has stimulated a concomitant initiative in the educational arena. In a series of so-called studies undertaken by professional women's groups in education the assertion has been made that girls may be getting short-changed. This allegation was made based upon the responses women made to a questionnaire as it related to their classroom experiences. In essence the study revealed that girls did not receive the same opportunities for participation in the classroom as did boys and, further, that teachers regardless of gender tended to discriminate against girls in terms of attention. Some studies maintained that girls' achievement levels were diminished by such actions causing them to lose status and ranking in their respective grades.

Perhaps the most controversial allegations made by certain factions within the educational community was that females learn differently than males and as a result are inherently at a disadvantage in certain academic disciplines such as science and mathematics. It is ironic that at a time when women are seeking and achieving equity throughout the socio-economic spectrum that some of their key representative organizations, such as N.O.W. and UPW, seek special treatment and privileged recognition because of their gender.

If boys receive more attention in class than girls it is more often than not due to misbehavior, although young women today seem to be achieving equity in that realm as well. This author's experience and observation recorded a wholly different gender problem. The females in my classes generally adapted to and took greater advantage of the numerous opportunities offered in school. A personal annual survey of area high schools by the author while still teaching consistently revealed that a distinct majority of valedictorians and salutatorians were of the feminine gender. Moreover, if anyone was willing to take the time to research the top ten percept of students in each grade classification within a geographically compact setting, the results would probably reveal a parallel pattern of female dominance.

It is my belief that greater harm is done to the so-called

women's movement when special treatment and/or legislation is promoted as a panacea for the centuries of inequality and second-class status rendered to women. As with affirmative action as it relates to cultural and ethnic minorities, both those people protected by special exception as well as those of the majority outside of the pale will always have doubts as to whether recognized ability and effort were sacrificed on the alter of political correctness. Was I recognized, hired, selected, awarded the position and/or honor due to my capacity and character or was it the result of an accident of nature such as skin color or gender?

This is the age of victimization wherein a variety of special interest groups identify themselves as victims of odious historical socio-economic customs and/or practices. They cry out for redemption and compensation for their ancestors' travails and their own perceived pains. In so doing they condemn themselves to the eternal self-doubt and frustration of never knowing whether they were really good enough to succeed on their own merit. Those in a position of authority within the educational community must not allow special interest groups based on gender, race, or class to dictate the course or substance of pedagogical progress. Faced with the current challenge to American educational status by a host of foreign school systems, we can ill afford the luxury of creating a class of individuals whose achievements were obtained more through legislation than by dedication.

In association with today's international competition with its common goal of creating and turning out an economically self-sufficient student, the issue of discipline rears its ugly head. Let us assume three types of discipline. First, and most important, there is self-discipline. This is the key to scholarship and successful lifetime accomplishment. It is characterized by the capacity to restrain and/or control those impulses and tendencies that distract us from the task at hand. In Confucian China it was equated with the virtuous man who conducted himself as society expected, not as his personal desires dictated. To the Japanese, it was the struggle between ninjo and giri, with the former dictating a course of action ruled by emotion while the latter imposing the restraint of duty and obligation to perform according to a social code of conduct.[6]

Second is the imposition by a higher authority of disciplinary measures. This form of discipline is characterized by the persona of the teacher and his/her capacity to instill within the disinterested minds of the student body the necessity and virtue of the learning process. Unfortunately, within today's American classroom, a teacher's effectiveness and quality of instruction lies less with his/her knowledge and background in the subject content and more with the ability to maintain and enforce discipline. This fact of academic life was brought home to this writer early in his teaching career. As a physical education major with a minor in history, I had reevaluated my primary career choice and had decided to seek employment and make a career within the social sciences. While fulfilling my student teaching requirements in physical education, a gentleman came into the gymnasium one day and proceeded to introduce himself to me as the Superintendent of Schools where I had applied for a position in the social studies department. He observed my then football-hardened, 230-pound frame, looked me in the eye and said, "You are going to make one helluva social studies teacher!"

I later learned in my pro-forma interview that the local school district was on probation within its interscholastic council for exhibiting less than civilized behavior when at home or on the road against its opponents. It was obvious that my brawn had been recognized as an effective agent for social and academic change within that specified school district.

Over the years it was my experience to see a number of fine teachers, some with brilliant minds and outstanding talents, driven from the classroom because of their inability to maintain discipline. In my early years, I ignorantly assumed an inherent incompetence on the part of those departed brethren. Later, as I became a veteran of the wars, a reevaluation of the circumstances surrounding their departure brought me to the sad conclusion that in order to survive in the American classroom one had to have an S.O.B. gene. What the hell is an S.O.B. gene, the reader may ask? Without going into a lengthy discourse, the S.O.B. gene bestows upon its owner that no crap will be tolerated and that if such is forthcoming then the instigators of same will be leaned on and there will be dire consequences for such recalcitrant behavior.

The establishment by the teacher at the outset of the school year of a clear and direct message, preferably in writing and reinforced orally, that both the students and teacher will be held accountable for their decorum and conduct within the classroom is mandatory. The teacher, as always, must set the example in terms of dress, language, and preparation. The student must not be allowed to experience a variety of discipline regimens wherein a smorgasbord of expectations are offered to choose and sample. As stated previously in this text, the American student is the toughest student in the world to teach. Like a young thoroughbred, our scholars must be trained and disciplined within a tightly constrained environment if they are to compete effectively with the other world-class schools. Discipline in the school systems of Japan, Taiwan, Israel, Singapore, France, and South Korea is not a variable that enters the equations of the learning process, it is a given! Therefore, the time and energy, not to mention the considerable resources devoted to remedial discipline, constitute an integral part of the American learning process and in so doing consume an inordinate portion of public funding for schools.

In Japan, the sensei spends zero time in establishing his status and authority. He/she just teaches! The same is true in all of the world class education systems. The discipline factor as I prefer to call it, enters into every decision that is made in the American public school whether the topic be grading, curriculum, testing, promotion, or homework. It is an incalculable factor which enters into the equation of the learning process defying statistical analysis in terms of its effect. A startling element involving the role of discipline in public education can be observed when one reviews the considerable amount of litigation that exists in our country regarding the issue of discipline and its role in directing the course of academic achievement. It is, therefore, incumbent upon the reader to comprehend that any discussion of student achievement or progress in the United States, grade levels K-12, must include the extent to which discipline or the lack thereof has made its presence felt.[7]

The third and most negative type of discipline in its application is that of remediation or behavioral readjustment in which the educational authorities through a limited variety of techniques attempt to, as the Maoists used to proclaim, reeducate the reactionary elements of society and show them the error of their ways. All school systems in the public sector by necessity have both extensive and legally articulate policy manuals on the subject of discipline and its enforcement. The legal basis for each punishment/penalty which is meted out for each infraction of an institution's rules and regulations has in general been carefully analyzed and researched relative to statutory and case law. All aspects of a regulation or rule are scrutinized in order to justify as Gilbert and Sullivan proclaimed, "...that the penalty fits the crime."

Having served over the years on almost every discipline committee ever organized by the school district it was always the incremental factor that consumed the bulk of our collegial efforts. Identification of the crime was easy, i.e., smoking, tardiness, insubordination, vandalism, etc. Matching the penalty to the violation of a rule or rules involved an incremental component which took into consideration a student's record or previous violations, circumstances concerning the instant offense, attitude of contriteness or belligerence, and external factors, such as home environment. Moving from the least penalty in severity to the greatest punishment inflicted was a limited theater of operations. Discussion by the Discipline Committee generally tended to be concentrated on the extreme end of the spectrum where speculation on the most effective instrument for terminating the illegal behavior in the shortest amount of time was of primary concern.

The scope of punishments were and are limited. Academic achievement and grades cannot be mingled with or affected by negative disciplinary behavior. The case law enforcing this precept is overwhelming. What can a school district do? The following is a list of what is legally available, within reason, as retribution to be applied to a recalcitrant scholar: detention after school or on Saturday, in-school suspension, loss of privileges (no free time, no passes from study hall), extended suspension of up to 5 days depending on the respective state, and, finally, expulsion from school on a long term basis. Long term expulsion involves a preliminary hearing wherein due process protections are invoked on behalf of the student who has right of counsel.

Within the academic community a philosophical dilemma prevails. Is it better to exclude or isolate the chronic violator from the rest of the student body by physically removing them from the school grounds or should school authorities create an alternative setting on school grounds where the disobedient student may be counseled and given instruction while serving time? Many school systems, especially in the urban areas, have created alternative learning centers. These are schools wherein troublemakers whose primary raison d'être is to challenge authority and refrain from any kind of purposeful learning are deposited. Those who advocate such a solution believe that contact with the educational system is preferable to non-contact under almost any circumstances. Since a large majority of this student-type brings a lot of baggage to school, such as: dysfunctional family, poverty, and criminal role models, the only stable and supportive experience for their day is the school!

The critics of alternate settings cite cost-benefit factors and the continued undermining of the public school's primary mission—academic achievement and preparation for acquiring a functionally successful role in society. The time, energy, resources, and excessive costs utilized in reorienting and reeducating the relatively small school population that refuses to practice socially and educationally acceptable behavior should lose the privilege of remaining at school. Those students who do practice and perform according to the school's stated mission should not be denied the scarce resources and funds that are redirected towards anti-social misfits whose consumption of same is out of all proportion to their numbers. Schools were never intended and they should not have been allowed to become the panacea for society's ills. In addition, these critics cite as evidence the historical spin-off of the socio-economic revolution of the 1960s which saw the public schools' administrative and instructional bodies mistakenly embrace the concept that our schools could absolve society of its responsibilities and resolve its problems. That, cry the critics, was the cardinal error that now manifests itself in a public school system which purports to be everything to everybody but in fact has spread itself too thin in order to meet its primary purpose—the preparation of a socio-economically and politically functional human being.

As always, the path of reasonable expectation lies somewhere between the two philosophies, with the most effective mix being currently experimented with inside the halls of Academe. This debate, as previously stated, is basically non-existent in all other world class school systems. That is the primary reason, in concert with a disastrously decentralized national school system, the United States is placed in a position of consistently trying to catch up to the competition.

It is important to understand the term baggage and its critical role in shaping student attitudes towards school. The increasing and alarming effect of the dysfunctional American family on the academic performance of its youngest members is critical. The acceptance by the public schools to execute the proxy of parenthood has become decisive. At the outset the necessary funding for such a Herculean task was readily made available both from the public and private sectors. In the typical American fashion it was accepted as an article of faith that if enough money was thrown at a problem in concert with good old American know-how any problem or obstacle to progress could be eliminated. The 1983 bomb-shell, A Nation at Risk, quickly dispelled this notion. Declining and/or stagnant SAT scores in association with poor results in international math and reading competition was sufficient fuel to arouse a formerly beneficent public into betrayed out-rage. What had happened to the money and the promises of academic excellence and achievement? A scapegoat was required and quickly identified as the educational establish-ment, i.e., administrators, teachers, and Boards of Education.[8]

Lost, forgotten, or conveniently ignored in the ensuing debate and finger-pointing has been the object of all the expressed concern and outcries of indignation—the students! The triumvirate of schools, government, and the public have made a dangerous assumption in this entire affair. Plainly stat-ed it is that the students are affected by the system but do not affect it. This supposition's weakness can be observed by an analogy in chemistry wherein all of the characteristic ingredi-ents in a chemical reaction are taken into account save one. The results, good or disastrous, cannot be effectively evaluat-ed as long as one of the ingredients remains excluded in the evaluative analysis. Thus it is with the present K-12 student body in America. Unlike their parents' and grandparents' generation, they have not been seen and unheard.

Today's students, especially in the 7-12 grade category, do have attitudes and a predisposition towards the learning process. Without taking these characteristic attitudes and dispositions into account within the equation of academic achievement we repeat the British error of omission on the eve of the Indian Mutiny of 1857. At a farewell gala given for the departing governor-general of India, Lord Dalhousie, the wife of the newly appointed governor-general inquired of the lady sitting next to her, who also was departing for

London's cooler clime, what knowledge of Indian culture she had acquired. The reply of the departing memsahib is illuminating. She stated unequivocally, "Nothing, thank God!" It is, therefore, imperative that we seek and take under advisement the perceptions and counsel of the 7-12 student body in the country. Their advice and suggestions are of the utmost value in the development of a responsive and proactive educational curriculum and organization for the 21st century. A note of caution, however, must be sounded if we are to avoid the mistakes of the 1960s. At that time the educational establishment, along with a large segment of American society, not only listened to but became willing apostles of those who protested the slings and arrows of their perceived outrageous fortunes. The lesson is clear, we must listen to our teen-age critics, for they have a degree of valuable input, but we must not as before allow the inmates to run the asylum.[9]

In this author's personal experience there have been a small but significant number of students whose perception, maturity, and acuity were substantial enough to be accorded absolute credulity. They have, however, been the exception and not the rule. For the overwhelming majority of students, the classic pattern of American conduct in school of minimal input and maximum expectation, is and has been the prevailing modus operandi. This attitude is the direct reflection of a society that minimizes effort and deferred gratification while simultaneously advocating/promoting immediate gratification through a network of strategically placed personal contacts. This code exists throughout our land, from the mean streets of East Los Angeles and Chicago's housing tenements into the boardrooms of corporate America. One's ability to move with ease and speed towards personal gratification with the least amount of effort is the socio-economic mantra of our time. After all it was the United States that invented fast food and the convenience store! Until endeavor becomes paramount over aptitude and effort is equated with success, American academic achievement will continue to languish and/or stagnate at the lower spectrums of international achievement.

Let us now turn our attention to another facet of the American public schools—athletics. Needless to say this subject occupies a special niche in the national psyche and exerts such a powerful influence on the attitudes and performance of our youth. In its purest form, the natural urge to compete, run, jump, throw, and kick is fundamental to human existence. However, the former pristine Olympic purpose of competition for the sake of participation and exerting the effort to momentarily reign triumphant has been somewhat altered. The activity itself and the collective and/or individual struggle which takes place within the competitive circle has become secondary to the persona, the athlete. In my undergraduate years as a physical education major we were taught that the act of participating in an athletic activity was ennobling in and of itself. Athletics were a means to an end, the development and enhancement of a sound and healthy body as complementary to an energetic mind.

Today, athletics, or sports if you wish, have become the end. This, of course, has been the direct result of the professionalization of athletics which bastardized its original purpose. The creation of a pantheon of national heroes was instituted not only as a source of income but as an inspiration and model for America's youth. At the outset there was at least an unspoken conspiracy between clubowners/management and the athletes themselves to present a positive image of heroic proportions. Despite their personal weaknesses and failings, the effort to effect a role model persona was consciously upheld. The Babe Ruths and Mickey Mantles, whose personal habits and appetites off the playing field were less than laudatory, nevertheless maintained a public image that allowed kids and their parents to have heroes who could be admired if not emulated. Although this author obviously reflects a generation gap and personal bias, it seems today that those individuals who occupy the pinnacle of athletic achievement and economic success are somewhat unappealing. Their undisguised contempt for fans, society, and even the law is discouraging to say the least. Those current professional athletes who do act civilly and maintain a positive image are given recognition no less, if not awards, for acting in a civilized manner. "Where are you, Joe DiMaggio?"

In many ways the professional athlete today, especially in baseball, football, and basketball, personifies all too many of the attributes which coaches in the public schools attempt to discourage—selfishness, disloyalty, bad language, non-sacrifice, and disdain for authority. This "hooray for me, the hell with you" attitude which the teenage competitor is confronted with on a constant basis creates within him/her a dilemma of major proportions. Should he/she listen to the coach who, in all probability, is being paid a pittance, or emulate the multimillion dollar behemoth who decries the inadequacies of his teammates, their management, the press, and the fans?

The immense sums of money lavished on professional athletes allows them to live in a style unknown to most Americans. The adulation given to them by adoring fans creates a harmony of illusion which is mistaken for reality by our youth. Athletics for too many becomes not just a path to economic success but unfortunately the only path to fame and riches.

For the inner city youngster it is the way out of his/her too often brutish existence. For the more affluent suburban youth it is the vehicle for a free ride or scholarship to the post-secondary institution of choice. What does this all mean? Well, for openers, it presents an alternative to academic achievement as the primary path to successful adulthood. Success in our society can be defined as achieving a degree of economic prosperity which allows an individual to become a conspicuous consumer of goods and services. With this in mind the reader can understand why the author is concerned with the comparative role, image, and status of the student and athlete.

Like his/her professional counterpart the student-athlete carriesa similar onerous burden: as role model to his/her peers. Unlike their vocational counterparts in the NBA or NFL/AFC, the high school athlete also carries a full-academic load. It is at this critical juncture, i.e., academics and athletics, that the pressure of a society's value-system is brought to bear. Must a choice be made between the two paths? Can the two paths complement each other and work in conjunction? It has been this writer's experience to observe that a significant number of athlete's over the years have been outstanding scholars *and* athletes. Despite the rigors of after-school practice sessions and in many cases an honors-level academic schedule these young men and women were capable of maintaining a high level of excellence in both arenas. Their formula was ultimately simple: expend maximum effort at all times in all endeavors. They were perfect role models for the entire student body. There was and is only one flaw in this portrait. Instead of serving as 'leaders of the masses' they too often became segregated, comprising an elite class, aloof and removed. The 'jocks's as other members of the studentbody referred to them as, unknowingly became clones of their professional counter-parts. In many ways they were silently disdainful of their lesser motivated and skilled brethren. After all, it was their effort and well-honed skills which had brought them to the level of success which they had brought them to the level of success which they had attained. The resulting schism has in some schools had negative manifestations leading to confrontation, isolation and in some cases physcial violence.

On a more positive if not questionable note, athletic team sports, especially those of football (the national passion), and basketball, have become the raison d'etre of neighborhoods and small towns/villages/cities. This is especially true in those municipalities and sub-divisions in which a prosperous economic past has been replaced by an aging population and an economic foundation with few if any positive future prospects. The high school athlete and the team become the vehicle by which past glories and successes are resurrected. The high school athlete in this environment becomes an icon, to be simultaneously exalted and lionized. Almost the entire populous becomes involved in some manner, directly or indirectly, with the organization and preparation for the local teams upcoming 'season.' Conversations at the local supermarket, diner, tavern, bowling alley, and veteran's halls all at sometime or another are concentrated on the prospects for a winning season. To the uninitiated outsider it appears somewhat ludicrous to observe so-called mature adults rationalize their existence upon the success or failure of the local football team.

What the non-believer is incapable of fathoming is the emotional appeal of identifying with a winner. Vince Lombardi summed it up perfectly: 'Winning isn't the most important thing; it is the only thing!' A community's pride and identity becomes synonymous with the rise and/or fall of their football or basketball team. An individual's desire to shout out to the world: 'I'm not a loser' manifests itself in the bleachers as he/she shouts encouragement and advice in an unashamed if not desperate association with a winner. The vicarious thrill of achievement which so-called adults attain through the athletic prowess of their sons and daughters is not experienced by the same constituency. Whereas, athletic contests and their participants receive the ultimate in publicity and active support throughout the year, those scholars of high academic standing are recognized only sporadically when honors students' names are published in local newspapers.

One high school known to this author attempted and succeeded briefly in somewhat reversing this pattern by instituting an Awards Assembly in which academic achievement and scholarship were exulted and those young scholars who had met the challenge of scholastic rigor were recognized. Time was taken out of the regular classroom schedule. Parents and relatives of the honorees were given ringside seats as they proudly watched their sons, daughters, nieces, nephews, and grandchildren have their moment in the sun as they strode to the auditorium stage to receive their awards. It was wonderful to observe the look on the faces of the recipients. It was even more gratifying to see the entire student body present and although the majority of them did not share in the enthusiasm of the recipients, it was crucial that they be there. In those two to three hours each spring, the entire mission and purpose of the school as an academic institution was realized.

But, alas, all good things come to an end, and so it was with the aforementioned Awards Assembly. The author learned that by a vote the faculty recommended this noble undertaking and demonstration of academic prowess be relegated to an evening, when the only members of the audience would be comprised of the honorees, their relatives, a few friends, and perhaps a few teachers and administrators. The irony of this decision is in its origins, the faculty. These people, who have been in the vanguard of protest of the lowering of standards and the non-recognition of scholastic achievement were the instruments of this enterprise's demise. How sad indeed!

What follows next is a series of profiles or representations of various student types which the author has encountered and/or observed over four decades. Some readers may perhaps recognize them.

The Scholar

A vanishing species whose numbers are either static or dwindling depending on one's geographic/socio-economic location. This student comes to school with the intent to learn and carries the expectation that teachers have come to teach. The scholar is generally more neatly attired and better washed and carries a backpack, gym bag in my day, containing all of the necessary materials/equipment for scholarly pursuit. Scholars are keenly, if not painfully, aware that they comprise a tiny minority in the building. Most, if not all, are scheduled into honors classes where they form an intellectual ghetto of sorts. In fact their entire day is spent in a ghetto-like existence segregated by choice from the commoners. They only contact a scholar has with the common folk is during lunch and in such classes as physical education, health, art, and/or music. The scholar has a full class load and in many instances the absence of any free period, even to eat. He/she functions under varying pressure from parents and friends of the same achievement level. The greatest pressure, however, comes from within. A scholar is as competitive for grades and evaluations as any athlete could ever hope to be.

Perhaps the most astonishing aspect of a scholar's existence in the American high school and the trait that has most impressed this author is the endurance and capacity to sustain a consistently high degree of motivational excellence within a sea of indifference and mediocrity. Often were the times when I wanted to apologize to them for having to tolerate the experiences of being in a building and/or classroom in which the quest for knowledge and truth as Gandhi understood it, was so painfully absent.

The Charmer, a.k.a. the Operator

This species presents an especially vexatious element within the context of pupil-teacher relationships. Teachers, as a group, are extremely vulnerable to praise and either consciously or subconsciously seek the approval of both their peers and students alike. This need for reaffirmation is our Achilles heel for it makes us easy prey for our modern-day Paris, the Charmer. He/she comes in all shapes/sizes/ages and from all socio-economic backgrounds. All varieties of this species share a single commonality—the capacity to ingratiate themselves to the evaluative authority of a teacher/administrator—through the process of captivating conversation and personality.

Charmers carefully evaluate and seek out victims. They will estimate which courses of study they have the least likelihood of either passing or obtaining a good grade in, and then proceed to cultivate a quasi-social relationship with that teacher. Time honored methods and routines include chatting with the teacher briefly before or after class on a variety of topics, remarking on the teacher's wardrobe and excellent taste thereof, commenting on how much he/she enjoys the class, and that Mr. X or Ms. Y is the best teacher they have ever had. Holidays afford the opportunity for a more material form of cultivation, with gifts or cards, although this has become rare.

The teacher, especially if a veteran, faces a familiar dilemma. Is Bobby Joe sincere in his words and/or actions or is this an attempt to curry favor and, henceforth, preferential treatment? The teacher's mindset wants to assume the best intentions on the part of any student but too many 'hits' over the years has brutalized him/her. The result in too many instances unfortunately is a tolerant but unimpressed audience. The Charmer, however, is seldom dissuaded and continues the assault. The teacher, depending on character, personality and experience, will more often than not allow the charade to continue but at a decreasing rate of interaction. The smart Charmer will know when to back off and seek out other prey. Urban youth are credited with being streetwise. Suburban/rural youth may add the dimension of being schoolwise.

The Slider

This variety of student is unfortunately increasing in number and in danger of rapidly becoming the average student. As the designation connotes the Slider slips through classes and academic responsibilities with a minimum of effort and interest. The scientific axiom of taking the path of least resistance is their credo. They generally harbor a subtle disdain for the educative process, blaming the tedium of curriculum, teachers, and administrators for their scholastic doldrums. In most cases the Slider is not a problem student insofar as discipline is concerned. An abhorrence of any activity which involves thinking and/or physical action preempts such behavior. A Teflon-like existence assures an academic career in which little to nothing will have any lasting effect in terms of life goals, assuming any are considered. To the Slider, Alfred E. Newman is an icon.

The Barbarian or Attila the Hun

The Hun, as we shall address this species, comes to school only because of legal mandates, and is frequently truant or tardy for classroom activity. Rules and regulations are there to be violated! A perfect school day for this archenemy of education consists of transgressing the maximum number of school regulations and either not getting caught or not being penalized if apprehended. The inordinate amount of energy, resources, and finances which are consumed daily in controlling and/or locating our Attila is mind-boggling.

The majority of this genre usually employ their barbaric skills outside of the classroom in the cafeteria and hallways. The remaining cohort take full advantage of any openings or weaknesses within and outside of the classroom. It is this latter element which is one of the major causative factors in retarding the progress of other less-minded students while simultaneously creating an environment which is less than conducive to the learning process.

The average amount of time allotted to a regular class is

40-50 minutes at the secondary level. This amount of time in and of itself is minimal, if not insufficient. With the presence of the Barbarian and his/her destructive behavior on exhibition, ten to fifteen percent on average of valuable classroom time can be wasted. What is of even worse consequence is when other borderline barbarians are induced to join the fray. The Utopian end sought is the total dismantling of the teacher's lesson plan and the satisfaction of being the instrument of its demise! What is even sadder about this scenario is the fact that in too many instances the students whose class time has been irrevocably stolen encourage through their silence or unconcealed amusement the continuation of this destructive behavior. Enter Brutus?

The Average Student or Joe and Jane Ordinary

This is the largest and most significant category of the student population. It is also the most distressing in terms of attitude and demonstrated effort. It is axiomatic that foreigners who come to the United States to observe our schools or be educated in them are almost unanimous in their observation that American students are not overly concerned or very serious about academic achievement. Academic success in terms of obtaining high grades has a low priority. Academic success in terms of passing or just getting by has a high priority. The effort necessary to obtain excellence is channeled into a variety of non-academic pursuits such as employment in order to buy clothes, automobiles, and insurance; cruising or hanging out; watching or playing sports; and watching television.

All students the world over consider themselves to be captive in the sense that they have been mandated to attend school and be educated. There is a natural reaction of rebellion on the part of any adolescent to such a condition. The nature and duration of this rebellion is what distinguishes the American student from their international counterpart. Joe and Jane Ordinary react by adopting the path of least resistance and settling into a rut of mediocrity for the greater part of their academic lives. This modus operandi is maintained primarily because school authorities, parents and society in general allow it. As mentioned previously in this chapter, Dickens' Pip can have no great expectations if none is demanded of him. So likewise is the case for our Joe and Jane. A pass/fail mentality permeates our academic community wherein success is equated with passing but not necessarily high grades. The reader is reminded that it is the so-called average student that is our greatest concern and not the scholar.

Low expectations have created a high middle cohort with relatively low self-esteem and a much reduced value in terms of how they perceive the relevance of their academic existence. Unlike the vast majority of other world class school systems where social pressure has made education the primary priority, Joe and Jane are bombarded with a Star Wars array of competing elements. Their focus becomes blurred and distorted as an increasingly permissive and amoral society allows them to dissipate their energies on material dead-ends such as professional sports, dating, sexual titillation, automobiles, etc. Perhaps, if we, the public, raised as much a hue and cry over the lack of a local Academic Booster Club as we do when a Sports Booster Club is non-existent we could then commence to reverse the descent into mediocrity and indifference which currently defines the average student's character. Peace!

Notes

1. *Schirokauer, 422-423.*

2. *Ibid., 436-437.*

3. *Patrick Smith, Japan: A Reinterpretation, (New York: Vintage Books, 1998), 75-77.*

4. *Education Week, "Quality Counts: A Report Card on the Condition of Public Education in the Fifty States," ed., Ronald A. Wolk, (Washington, D.C.: Editorial Projects in Education, Inc., 2997), 155-157.*

5. *Charles Dickens, Great Expectations, (Milwaukee: Raintree, 1989), 98-100.*

6. *Schirokauer, 29-31.*

7.*Ibid., 372.*

8.*National Commission on Excellence in Education, A Nation at Risk: The Imperative for Educational Reform, (Washington, D.C.: Government Printing Office, 1983), 10-12.*

9.*Percival Spear, India: A Modern History, (Ann Arbor: The University of Michigan Press, 1961), 226-227*)

Chapter Six

The Parents

6

Parents: "Hooray for my kid, the hell with yours!"

Perhaps the most significant metamorphosis that has taken place in the educational arena has been that of the role of the parent. Since the roaring sixties the generally acquiescent and supportive parent of the pre-sixties has been replaced by a generally active, if not critical, parental model who seeks and/or demands a participatory role in the formal education of their children.

At one time parents, usually the mother, were content to serve on PTA committees, act as class/grade parents in the elementary schools or, if the spirit moved them, run for and sit on the local Board of Education/School Committee. Although this form of participation still continues unabated, an additional and more profoundly involved parental partnership has emerged. This new partnership, as it is perceived by parents, involves an equal role in the management of schools, selection of texts, formulation of curricula, and the selection and evaluation of instructors. This collective urge to quasi-administer the public schools was given an added impetus in 1983, with the much heralded, A Nation at Risk. For many parents, any lingering doubt which they may have had regarding the quality of their children's education was exponentially elevated.[1]

Before the reader assumes that the author is intimating and/or proposing that the good old days of benign parental involvement are preferred or longed for, let it be stated unequivocally, "NOT SO!" It has indeed been the undeniable and uncontested fact of the matter that the lack of direct and active parental involvement in the education of their off-spring has been the major contributor to the problems that the public schools currently struggle with. We will not bore the reader with the statistical and oft-cited evidence of the deterioration and decline of the influence of the family in American life. With the reluctance of stating the obvious, it is axiomatic that a society that produces a significant cohort of dysfunctional families cannot hope to expect that its educational system, a governmental entity, could act as an effective surrogate in the raising of its children. Yet, that is exactly what was and has been expected.

In the Pontius Pilate-oriented society of America today, we hypocritically proclaim the necessity of providing the best quality education for our children while simultaneously demonstrating an unrelenting quest to reduce the cost of doing so. This inherent contradiction is mirrored within the context of our familial dynamics wherein parents expect the best out of their off-spring while attempting to reduce the cost in terms of personal involvement in the attainment of such excellence.

Parents today constitute an interest group which has experienced an intriguing historical journey. Their organizational framework has taken them from the benign PTA/class-room mother advocates of public education to the status of critical evaluators of the educational delivery system. Although such participation is not in and of itself negative or unwarranted, it can be destructive when its objective is the personal aggrandizement of parents for the sake of one child. The collective responsibility of the educational bureaucracy towards all students is challenged by the selfish requests/demands of parents who see the schoolhouse as an entity existing solely for the immediate gratification of their child's wants and needs.

The trend towards the individualization of the educative process became fully realized in the post-1960s era, when the existentialist ideal became the philosophical mantra of the moment. The egoistic foundations of our nation's current debate on educational priorities and/or programs were laid at this time. Alexandre Dumas' rallying cry voiced by the Three Musketeers, "One for all," was preempted and radically diminished by the remaining portion of the cry, "...and ALL for ONE," by many parents. What would have been scoffed at by the greater American public before the 1960s was now taken for granted as education's new guiding principle.[2]

The natural outcome in the future of such a self-serving credo can and will be the establishment of an Individualized Education Plan (I.E.P.) for each student, K-12. Such plans, as mentioned previously, exist today primarily within the realm of special education. The special needs and requirements of this special student population mandate such a disposition of educational services. It may well be that parents of non-special education children, aware of the considerable extra expenditure reserved for special education students, feel short-changed. Perhaps they feel that their children are special also and should be treated as such. The manifestation of this "my kid is special" syndrome is the I.E.P. wherein an individually tailored program for every student is constructed in order to meet their unique qualities and needs. This can and probably will involve not only course selection, but teacher preference, guidance/ psychological service preference, and school building preference.

The argument for such a district-wide education plan becoming a recipe for dissension, confrontation, and possible litigation is compelling. Teachers will be pitted against teachers. Parents will be pitted against parents. Boards of Education, seeking a philosophical middle ground, will satisfy no one and be accused by all of not allowing each child to be all that he/ she can be.

In this author's opinion it is this attitude, as stated in the title of this chapter, that poses the greatest threat to the public school system in its current form. As parents increasingly perceive the schools to exist primarily for the exclusive utilization of their off-spring (although they will deny such a motive) their dissatisfaction will also increase when their desires are not realized. The causes of the dissatisfaction are more often than not inconsequential in nature and judgmental at best. An illustrative list would include grading of term/ research papers, too much homework, insufficient assignments for students on vacation when school is in session, insensitive administrators/ teachers not in tune with special needs of children, lack of discipline (usually on the part of the student whose parents are making the claim), to mention a few. The unhappy parents, if their demands are not met, will generally add a fiscal factor at this point, namely that their taxes (believed always to be too high) are not being used effectively and, therefore, some form of remedial action is required. Enter the watchdog community organization which proceeds to inform the community that mischief is afoot!

The issue or issues are defined, a phone chain established, a meeting is scheduled (usually at the residence of the organizer), and those of a similar persuasion gather to express their concern and/ or outrage over the perceived injury or inadequacy of the school system. An acronym is usually created in order to increase visibility. Some forms of the attention getting acronyms can be APE (Advocates for Personal Education), ASS (Advocates for Superior Students), KISS (Knowledge Is Self-Satisfying), or PISS (Parents In Search of Success). Not all parental-inspired organizations are negative. Although in a minority, a number of such groups are supportive of the schools and usually appear as a reaction to the anti-school element. They, too, enter into the contest or war of acronyms. They may include SOS (Save Our Schools), YES (Youths Emerge Successful), and OSAGE (Our Schools Are Great Educators).

Once these groups go public the fun really begins. Advocates from both sides of the issues take up arms and use the media, lawn posters, Board of Education meetings and/or specially organized forums to argue and demonstrate on behalf of their respective positions. The process can, and often does, become quite ugly with accusations and counter-accusations being hurled at each other. As in any political contest the battle and propaganda are waged in order to claim the support of the silent and somewhat ignorant majority! Parental support is critical to the warring factions because they generally are the voters who will eventually decide the issue by electing those members of the most convincing faction to lead the school district as Board of Education members. If the issues are hot enough, e.g. teacher salaries/contracts, athletics, tax levies, discipline, or uniforms, then the effort to involve people and raise their passion will be maximized. The key to seizing control of a Board of Education by any self-interest group is to identify the prejudices of the community and expand on them within an educational context. One example is parent dissatisfaction with individual teachers gets translated into an anti-union issue.

As oft-cited in this text, the seeds of dissatisfaction with the current edition of public education were sown in the 1960s. Since then, the pursuit of immediate self-gratification on a universal basis and the simultaneous rejection of deferred gratification at the communal level has created the perfect environment for discord and discontent. The educational community in a miscalculated attempt to meet the demands of a parental generation steeped in self-aggrandizement made promises that it could not keep. Chief among those promises was the de facto guarantee that given an adequate and continuous supply of funding at both the federal and state levels, each child would be given both the opportunity and realization of achieving academic success within the limits of his/her ability. Neither the educational bureaucracy or the community at large realistically comprehended the dimension of that pledge.

The collective and cooperative effort necessary to come even close to achieving the goal sought never manifested itself. All parties to the competition sought to achieve their personal objectives in a self-serving manner. For the educators—administration, teachers, and teacher unions—it meant knowing what was best for the schools. For the parents, it meant seeking to have the entire system geared to the want/needs of their individual children. For the community, concerned primarily with the level of funding necessary to support an educational system that burdened them with an unduly perceived harsh tax levy, it meant tax relief.

The national perception today is that our public schools have failed in their mission to qualitatively educate our youth.

This has provided the fuel for parental empowerment. Using the private schools as leverage for greater parental involvement, schools throughout the nation are becoming hostages to various cliques whose modus operandi is to make parents unhappy. The organization and establishment of a phalanx of angry parents is carefully nurtured in order to make the watchdogs' objectives appear to be identitical with that of the parental cohort. Therefor, those groups who would implant their religious, sexual, gender, racial, and/or economic convictions within the context of educational governance unfortunately have an all too-willing parental constituency.

Chalker and Haynes state unequivocally that any evaluation of a world class school can have real meaning only when the hypotheses that positive parental influence and a stable and caring home environment accompanied by a supportive community are accepted as the critical determinants of success in school. In their research on world class standards for involvement in the education process, they present the assumption that adult literacy reflects the value placed on education within the home. If this assumption is valid then it would proceed that completion of schooling would be a high priority. If such is the case, then a more literate society would insist on, if not guarantee, a successful school system. It follows, therefore, that literate parents want literate children. What happens when illiterate parents want literate children? When this latter home environment exists, then an artificial and fragile learning experience is realized by the child because the reinforcement factor so necessary to sustained and effective learning is depreciate beyond the point of redemption. Literacy and successful academic achievement become estranged from one another, leading to frustration and disappointment in both parents and children alike. Clearly, if a child/student is taught in school that reading literacy is fundamental to academic success and then returns home each day to find little if any literary activity—newspaper, magazine, or book reading taking place—a contradiction has been created. This more subtle type of parental involvement is overlooked or undervalued too often in terms of its effect on the educative process. It is fundamental to academic success.[3]

Chalker and Haynes suggest and offer the establishment of an education ethic that would set the tone for parents and children to interact with each other. They list eight crucial activities which would be required of all parents and/or significant adults in a child's life.

1. Maintaining high and realistic expectations for a child in school.

2. Consistent disciplining of a child at home so that he/she can accept and exhibit discipline at school.

3. Creating a love of learning.

4. Creating a love of reading by reading to the child and serving as a model by self-reading.

5. Establishing education as a natural prerequisite for success in life.

6. Teaching the child that real success is a result of hard work.

7. Teaching the child that teachers deserve and require respect.

8. Teaching the child that effort, not ability, is the cornerstone of success.[4]

Obviously, the reader could add other items of value to the list which might have a positive impact on the attitudes of parents/children. If such an itemized list were posted in a conspicuous place in each home and given an honored presentation by framing it it would be interesting to speculate on the effect it might have upon student work ethics and achievement. So much for wishful thinking.

What follows next are composite caricatures of parents and/or guardians which the author has encountered over the years and who have made the educational environment a minefield for the unwary.

The Critic

This species of parent has become since the mid-seventies one of the most prolific breeders in terms of numbers in the country. The critic has always had an agenda and lengthy list of grievances which have been festering over the years. This species can be recognized in one of the following forms. There is the senior citizen who feels the country is going to hell in a hand basket and blames the schools for either causing and/or doing little to correct society's increasing supply of teenage profligates. The professional, usually a lawyer, engineer, or self-made man/woman considers teachers and/or administrators as second class citizens and basically incompetent. Lastly, there is the sub-type who feels that the instructional staff, curriculum, administration, bus transportation, school facilities, textbooks, guidance services, medical services, and color of the carpet are inadequate to the task of effectively educating his/her treasure, i.e., child.

Whatever the configuration, all critics share one attribute and that is: they can never be satisfied. The secret of course is that they don't really want to be satisfied. Each critic harbors and nourishes a grievance which has its origin in an event within the educational setting which has caused them and/or their children to be somehow irreparably harmed. The incident or person that triggered the critic into action may very well have been of a relatively minor nature. In most cases the redress and/or response to the critics demands are perceived by him/her as totally inadequate and as an attempt by school authorities to cover-up and deny the alleged wrong.

The author is not attempting to paint all critics of the schools with the same brush. There are many constructive suggestions and changes proposed by critics of the schools who should and must be given credence. This species in my experience has been a minority because they actually want to improve, assist, and participate in the construction of a vibrant and renewed public school system. The critic in the title role of this caricature has few such ennobling intentions in mind. The end sought by him/her is the privatizing of the educational system in order to achieve some mystical national standard of achievement which never really existed in our history.

The Elementary Parent: Show and Tell

Of all parental configurations, the elementary species is probably more directly and intimately involved with their offspring's education than any other type. This is only natural due to the novelty and fundamental concern for this age group's, i.e., five to eleven years old, need for establishment of sound and effective learning habits. The novelty aspect is self-evident—the daily arrival of homework assignments and school activities will require much larger refrigerators in the future to post little Moe's and Maude's handiwork. The relief at placing them on the school bus each day is exceeded only by the O's and E's (outstandings and excellents) that fill every nook and cranny of the report card and/or anecdotal report. The incremental progression of the child's achievement serves as a stimulus to parental involvement in most cases. The committees/events which fill the school calendar allow for ample parental participation. Birthday parties, homeroom mother/father, flea market spectacular, sports days, and special events all serve as modern-day sirens on the rocks for the willing parent. But it's fun, and you can still enjoy being around your kids and sharing their unsophisticated love for learning as they discover their ever-expanding universe and the intricacies of creating six-pointed snowflakes.

The Secondary Parent: No News is Good News

The nostalgia for the good old days, i.e. the elementary years, increases exponentially as Moe and Maude continue their odyssey through middle and secondary school. The novelty has long since worn off and the excitement of viewing your cherubs' school work and/or meeting his/her teachers has been replaced by the semi-dread of such an encounter. The fridge's door is almost empty and devoid of any evidence of educational achievement. In its place we observe a calendar of household assignments and extracurricular school activities which would be the envy of a Port Authority transportation supervisor. Instead of eagerly awaiting and looking forward to news from school, the absence of any such daily communication is greeted with a collective sigh of relief by the parents.

The intensity of the competition for grades within an increasingly sophisticated body of subject matter creates a low voltage struggle within the household as parental expectations and student achievement too often may move in opposite directions. The close, supportive and intimate relationship of the elementary years has been replaced by a more hesitant and doubtful demeanor. Although not seeking an adversarial relationship, the secondary parent, due partly to media bombardment and partly to a feeling of inadequacy, increasingly comes to look upon the education institution as less than a partner and more as an emotionless governmental body which must be carefully scrutinized and monitored.

This circumstance is no one's particular fault. It is the nature of the beast. All the hallmarks of a democratic capitalist society—competition, recognition of ability, seizing opportunity, personal fulfillment, immediate gratification, and emphasis on individual achievement create a milieu that guarantees a relationship of tension due to 'great expectations.' Add to this mixture, the college for everyone syndrome and it is not difficult to comprehend the metamorphosis of the parent from homeroom Mom to the doubting Thomas.

The Expert: Knows All, Sees All!

Over the years of being a classroom teacher perhaps no other parental species brought out any latent homicidal tendencies in me more than the expert. The stereotypical profile generally consisted of a male parent with professional background in the physical sciences and more often than not a New York State bureaucrat of middle to upper level status. Also included within this category was the male entrepreneur or successful businessman. The common thread which joined all experts together was their inherent low voltage contempt for teachers and the educational establishment.

The expert could be expected to appear in a cloud of smoke at regular intervals such as Board of Education meetings at budget time, parent-teacher conferences, and, of course, at Open House nights. It seems that the larger the audience, the greater the motivation for our expert to expound upon educational theory/practice and illuminate our otherwise unenlightened lives. He was an individual who had obviously done some reading on the subject, had probably observed a Robert Bennett PBS special on the topic, and held as his canon of belief the 1983 thriller, A Nation at Risk. In conjunction with the preceding qualities it was always this author's conviction that deep beneath the expert's outward layer of disdain dwelled a frustrated teacher wannabe! How else could you explain the expert's consistent and almost maniacal penchant to instruct and guide his audience, especially when they were teachers and/or administrators.

What is the expert's problem? Fundamentally, the expert has been indoctrinated by certain external forces which have convinced him that the members of the educational establishment are really a bunch of amateurs who are relatively unsure as to how, when, and why children learn. As a reinforcement to this belief, the expert looks upon unions as the agent which insulates the body of amateurs from the reality of the marketplace and, henceforth, accountability.

This author has always felt that the so-called expert, sometime in his past, suffered a traumatic experience in his formal education and has in some convoluted manner used this experience as a springboard for his/her attitudes toward teachers and teaching. The basis for this impression comes from four decades of parent-teacher conferences and open houses where in the course of a discussion allusions to incidents and events in the course of a parent's schooling were subtly revealed. The expert more often than not can be depended upon to vote down the school budget and be a staunch advocate of free choice in the selection of a child's place of schooling. I also suspect that Rush Limbaugh may be considered by the expert to be a candidate for a Pontifical office.

The Helpless Parent: I can't do anything with them

Perhaps no other parental species awakens the chords of sympathy and futility more than the parent who in desperation seeks solace and/or solutions to familial and academic problems from school authorities. The incremental factor in this unfortunate condition became more noticeable and established from the 1970s onward. The increasing incidences of parental frustration and anguish in dealing with their children at home was a primary focus in the increasing frustration experienced by teachers in the classroom. If the teacher could not utilize the home as an effective means of reinforcing the schools' rules/regulations and expectations, then the control factor became neutralized. By control factor we mean the element of student expectations in which certain kinds of negative behavior would elicit predictable and consistent responses from both the home and school.

When I first began my teaching career the control factor was firmly in place and well-established with both the school and parents generally reciprocating similar expectations. In those early days of the 1960s parents expected, if not demanded, teachers and administrators to be not only instructors but disciplinarians as well, and they backed and supported the school authorities in the rendering of such action. Then something changed. The doubtful and challenging parent replaced the supportive and assured parent. The incremental demise of the American family and Dr. Spock have received much attention and criticism for the change in attitudes toward child-rearing. I'm not sure whom or what was to blame. The results, however, were quite evident as manifested in the negative and/or indifferent attitude that became the hallmark of much of the student body.

As the schools became more and more challenged by the disruptive, inattentive and indifferent behavior of an increasing number of students, support from the parental authority was eagerly sought. In too many cases it was not forthcoming; not because the parents refused to cooperate but because they could not cooperate. When contacted by a teacher or principal or guidance counselor, the unrelenting refrain which emerged from the home was, "We can't do a thing with him/her. We were hoping that the school could come up with something." The recurring lament of these parents was vividly described as they related their incapacity to influence and direct their children's behavior. In many instances the pleas for help came from a single-parent household, usually the mother, although in recent years the gender factor has been less influential.

The helplessness of parents in dealing with the exhibited academic and/or disciplinary indifference of their offspring was demonstrated most shockingly in those stories in which the child or children established as well as dictated the manner and mode of the family's daily routine. In order to avoid confrontation on any and all issues, the parental authority submitted to the wishes and demands of the junior members of the family. The control factor had effectively been transferred from the adult to the juveniles. Where did this leave the schools? "We stand at Armageddon, and battle for the Lord!" (Thanks, T.R.)

Notes

1.National Commission on Excellence in Education, A Nation at Risk: The Imperative for Educational Reform, (Washington, D.C.: Government Printing Office, 1983), 10-12.

2.Alexandre Dumas, The Three Musketeers, ed. Frank N. Magill, (Englewood Cliffs: Salem Press, 1976), 320-323.

3.Donald M. Chalker and Richard M. Haynes, World Class Schools: New Standards for Education, (Lancaster: Technomic Publishing Co., Inc., 1994), 187-188.

4.Ibid., 191.

Chapter Seven

Pilgrims Progress

7

Pilgrim's Progress: A Unionist's Sojourn

I f school officials—Superintendents, Boards of Education members, principals—in a moment of candor were to be queried regarding the least palatable event of the past forty years, I am sure that a majority would suggest the passage of the Taylor Law in 1967. On the opposite side—teachers and all other public employees—the passage of the Public Employees Fair Employment Act was hailed as a much over-due piece of legislation analogous in many ways to the Declaration of Independence or Magna Carta. Although an imperfect statute and in a number of critical areas (e.g., no-strike clause) seriously flawed it nonetheless placed the destiny of the employees firmly within their own hands for the first time.

It will not be the intent of this chapter to analyze and review the history of this legislation and the ensuing case law and decisions since its passage. It is, however, the author's intent and objective to describe the evolution of the teacher movement through the eyes and experience of one of its par-ticipants who acted in a leadership role. With the teacher union movement as a suitable backdrop, the author will describe his 26 years of experience and metamorphosis as a union man.

My first appointment to a probationary position was as a

social studies teacher of American history, grade eight. The school district was in a small rural upstate New York village where everyone knew everyone as well as their business. My roots as a teacher were planted there. I was also hired as an assistant football coach. It was 1960, I was single and earning the grandiose sum of $4,500 per year. In those days the leader/president of the local teacher/educator unit was generally the principal who collected our dues and urged us to join the statewide organization as well. Once a year in October, a regional conference was held at the capitol in Albany. It was usually held on a Friday in the Palace Theatre where a keynote speaker addressed a few thousand educators with what were generally some forgettable words of wisdom. This, of course, was after a half to three-quarter hour wait for Mayor Erastus Corning to greet us on stage and serve as a further cure for insomnia. Many teachers usually used this day as a long weekend sans Albany.

It was during these early years of 1960-66 that teachers as a class were generally apolitical when it came to labor-management relations. Compensation and related benefits were of primary concern. Class size, personal leave days, grievance process/arbitration (what was that?), length of the school year/day, etc. were outside the realm of consideration. These terms and conditions of employment were determined by the gods which in this case was the Superintendent of Schools and Board of Education members. The older teachers were the unhappiest over their employment conditions but had conceded a long time ago that to rock the boat was in no one's best interest, least of all theirs.

It was during my second educational experience that the steel was forged which would inevitably lead to my involvement and active participation in the national union movement. I spent but one year in this second school district, located in the suburbs of Rochester, New York. It was not a pleasant experience! The good old days of my initial labors in the Gardens of Academe were essentially wiped out. From a semi-Utopian environment where respect for teachers and their craft was almost universal, I had entered an environ of confrontation and adversarial relations wherein both students and administrators perceived teachers and me as less than their equals.

Both the principal and my department chair were of the same mind in terms of their attitudes towards me. I was too independent and had to be remolded to fit their image of a probationary teacher. I received between ten and fifteen classroom observations collectively from both gentlemen during the first two months of school. The usual number per annum is three or four for probationers and one or two at most for tenured personnel. My reputation as a disciplinarian and no-nonsense teacher was obviously of minor consequence within the scheme of things. My classroom performance was deemed mediocre by my department chair because I lectured too much and refused to allow the students to run the class. The diminutive principal, who had the annoying habit of bouncing on his toes when speaking to you, felt that I was too hard on the children as he referred to the six-foot tall semi-barbarians who delighted in disrupting classes and generally raising hell. Both of these academicians wanted to get rid of me. They evidently had never come up against a non-tenured, first year teacher who pedagogically practiced what he believed in and would not compromise any of his principles.

Before the principal could fire me, he left the district for a Superintendency at another school district. His replacement, the assistant principal, who had obviously been briefed about the beast in Room 22, paid me a visit in the form of a formal classroom observation. A large, affable man of southern Mediterranean heritage, he handed me my observation with the comment, "I have never observed anyone who used the chalkboard as masterfully as you do!" In the post-observation conference in his office he offered me a $500 raise to stay on in the district, commenting at the conclusion of the meeting, "We need more people like you on the faculty." I thanked him for his offer and much needed support, but clearly stated my future plans in education did not include a continuation in my present place of employment.

At this juncture the reader may be wondering why the preceding narrative of the author's experience in his second place of employment is pertinent to his genesis as a union activist. It is quite simple. I was rudely awakened to the fact that at no time during that hellish year was there anyone or any organization that I could look to for real support or succor. As a first year probationer I was left alone dangling gently in the breeze with my career being determined by individuals who I either did not respect or was helpless to effectively defend myself against. As Scarlet O'Hara in that now famous scene at Tara, vowed, "I will never be poor again!" For me, it meant the poverty of the legitimate means to obtain professional independence and security.

It was at my third and what proved to be my last tenured position of public school employment that my avocation as a union activist and leader was established. My direct involvement in the union movement did not come until my second year in the school district. My involvement came about in a rather intriguing way. A fellow colleague had been after me to attend a general meeting of the local teachers' association. I finally succumbed to his entreaties and joined him at what would prove to be the first of many, many union meetings that would follow over the ensuing years. At this particular meeting, which pre-dated the Taylor Law, the teachers' salary committee was making a presentation on the schedule of monetary requests that it would present to the Board of Education. As I sat there listening to the monotonous and uninspired discourse of the salary committee's chairman, the revelation came to me that this person was not going to represent me at a Board of Education meeting. Hell, if I was a Board member I wouldn't give the teachers a raise either based solely on the drabness and lack of enthusiasm of its uninspired presenter.

Before the teachers' association meeting adjourned the president invited any members in attendance who might be interested to join the salary committee. It was at that moment that yours truly became a union activist and proceeded to rush to the podium to enlist. As a sidelight, the reader might be interested to know that the chairman of the salary committee, whose uninspired and witless presentation was a catalyst for my active entry into the union, later became and elementary principal. His tenure as such was equally as uninspiring.

Following the aforementioned general meeting, the salary committee met to plot its strategy and prepare for its presentation to the Board of Education. Although I was technically not a member of the Association, my impassioned commentary on the importance of the teacher to American society influenced a majority of the committee to the extent that I was asked to draft a written proposal that would be submitted to the Board of Education. Motivated by the euphoric success of my conquest of the salary committee and self-impressed with my own rhetoric, I quickly proceeded to write an eleven page magnum opus. The gist of the papal encyclical was an appeal to the better angels of their nature of the Board of Education who were requested to give the teachers a $200 increase in their salaries in recognition of their long-standing contribution to the advancement and success of the District's children. The encyclical was distributed to the Board members for their consumption prior to the meeting.

What followed next removed any doubts which I may have harbored regarding my newly self-ordained ministry in the union movement. Our contingent of Association representatives was made to wait until after the regular Board meeting had concluded three hours later. At that time the Board president formally recognized our presence and inquired as to whether we had any additional comments to make in support of our salary proposal. As he spoke those words, two members of the Board got up from their seats, went to the coat rack, and proceeded to leave the meeting, making comments to the effect of, "...overpaid, under-worked people..." Their looks of contempt and utter lack of civility was and still is burned indelibly into my mind. We did not get a raise that year.

From that night onward my professional course of action was set. I would do all that my physical and mental energies would allow to erase the contempt and second-class status which my colleagues and I had endured on that infamous evening. The good news came in 1967 with the passage of the so-called Taylor Law or Public Employees Fair Employment Act. It was and is the public employees' Emancipation Proclamation. Although imperfect and with a sizeable wart, i.e., no-strike clause, this hallmark legislation accomplished what the Wagner Act of 1935 had done for the private sector. It mandated employer recognition of and entry into collective bargaining agreements with duly certified labor organizations.[1]

Our education association, as it was called in those early years, since the word union offended too many of its members, went about preparing for its maiden voyage at the bargaining table. Our statewide organization held training sessions for the 700-plus school districts. The state organization was as new to such activity as the locals were. As I look back on the 1960s and 1970s, a smile comes to my face as I recall some of the preparation and organization that our negotiating team, or "The Boys" as we came to be known, experienced. One of the more amusing if not illuminating events occurred when a local/regional meeting was called by the State Teacher's Association in order to afford the various union locals the opportunity to mingle with each other and build a kind of esprit de corps. Each local unit was asked to introduce itself and briefly relate some of its thoughts/ideas and reactions regarding the newly established labor-management relations environment. The president of one of the smaller school district teachers' association stood when his turn came and proceeded to introduce members of his district's Board of Education! He then stated, to a rather stunned and if not somewhat amused audience, that due to the exceptionally positive relationship which the Teachers' Association and the Board of Education shared with each other, that the Taylor Law would probably have little to no effect on existing labor-management relations. Future events in that particular school district did not prove to reflect that president's optimism or prediction.

At the historic initial meeting between the two negotiating teams in our district, the Board's team, consisting of an amalgam of administrators, including the Superintendent of Schools and Business Manager, as well as Board of Education members, faced off against the teachers' team consisting of four secondary teachers i.e. Science and Social Studies equally represented. Our team had been instructed by the state union to have each member assigned to a specific task. One individual was to be chief spokesman or negotiator who would do the talking. A second member would take notes on the evening's proceedings. A third member was to be a watcher and observe signals or tendencies that the other side was exhibiting. The fourth member was to assist the chief negotiator by passing notes from himself and/or members of the team regarding any points in the discussions which should be added, clarified, changed, and/or expanded upon. Since all four of us could have been the chief negotiator, his role frequently required the calling of caucuses in order to quell and/or control the other three musketeers.

The Board's chief negotiator was its President, who considered himself somewhat in a liberal vein and who proved to be an intelligent and eloquent opponent. He created at the outset a perception that he was extremely knowledgeable in education law and its application. In numerous instances, when the teacher's team proposed a clause or choice of wording for inclusion in the projected agreement, the Board president would look at us forlornly and say, "Gee, fellas, we would like to agree to that wording but it is in violation of Education Law." We would then, more often than not, dejectedly call for a caucus. Upon our return to the table, our chief spokesman would state, "We'll get back to you on that." One evening during the negotiations, after declaring his oft-quoted apology, one of our team members suddenly asked, "What law are you referring to?" The Board president's look of dismay accompanied by the lack of his usual riposte to our queries caused a collective doubt to be raised in our minds as to his knowledge of education law. That was the night we grew up!

The reader must appreciate the fundamental factor which affected the initial year of collective bargaining; and that was that a bi-laterally agreed upon document had to be created from scratch. The document, i.e. the Agreement or Contract, had to be developed from the cooperation of two diametrically opposed forces. One force, the Board of Education, held the cards so to speak. Prior to the Taylor Law, they had held all of the trump cards and had dictated the rules of the game. The other force, the teachers, with utopian hopes/ideas had the onerous task of wresting the deal, naming the game, and designating trump from the Board. We learned collectively, individually, and very quickly that it would take more than one year to even the playing field. In retrospect, it actually took two decades.

Much has been written on the history of the labor-management relations in the private sector. The library shelves are replete with the sad history of the confrontational and adversarial relationship which has existed in the United States between labor and management. The historical odyssey of the labor movement in the public sector however is in its infancy. It is with pride that this author participated as a midwife of sorts through its birth and adolescence. The reader is asked to indulge the author in his reminiscences of the natal labor movement in the public sector. The hurdle that public employees had to overcome was established early on when then Governor Calvin Coolidge stated during the Boston Police strike of 1919, that, "No one has the right to strike against the public welfare at any time." Thereafter, a stigma was attached to the very act if not the idea of a teacher, fireman, or policeman withholding his services from a municipality or other public entity. Thus, a second-class citizenship of sorts was firmly established in the history of our nation. Such inferior bargaining status spilled over with varying degrees into other employment sectors as well, such as nursing, medical doctors, hospital workers, and public works employees to name a few. The horrifying image of a child's teacher on strike and/or carrying a picket sign in public was only amplified by the general public's concomitant horror of witnessing its medical establishment refusing to render its services while also carrying picket signs in front of a staffless hospital. The general public's reaction to private sector work stoppages, although finding them inconvenient, was looked upon as a necessary evil to be endured and tolerated.The myth of the absolute necessity of preventing/barring workers in sensitive and critical public service jobs from voluntarily withdrawing their services has since become an axiom in labor-management relations.

What is generally not understood by the lay public, and some union members for that matter, is that the most critical aspect of a collective bargaining agreement is not its creation or modification but its enforcement. In many ways over the years this dictum served to be a guiding light in the conduct of my avocation as a union activist. More by accident than by intent, the final metamorphosis of my union activism took place with my involvement as a member and then as chairperson of our Association's Grievance Committee.

In the early days of the public sector's fledging union movement, the role of grievance processing and its effect on employees' terms and conditions of employment was not fully appreciated or strategically perceived. Everyone understood or at least felt that they comprehended the collective bargaining process and its outcome, the Agreement. For the vast majority of union members the conclusion of negotiations and the signing by both parties to the Agreement was the apex of union activity until the next round of collective bargaining. In the initial years, i.e. the 1960s, this meant annual contracts with negotiations taking place every 9-12 months! It wasn't until the 1970s that multi-year agreements were inaugurated. This is an indication to the reader of the novice nature of the collective bargaining process that existed at the time in the educational arena. The collective bargaining process in many ways made the grievance process a step-child of sorts. The naivete of the teachers and their unions was at least party responsible. In their neophyte stage they had made the assumption that both parties would live up to the word and the spirit of the Agreement. What they would quickly and ofttimes painfully experience was the shattering fact that the other party was not necessarily prepared to do so. It came as somewhat of a shock to many members of the instructional staff (they did not look upon themselves as union members) when their grievance chairman (not the author) made his initial report in 1968 to our executive committee that the District was allegedly in violation of three of our members' Rights under the recently signed Agreement. So much energy and effort had been devoted to the creation of a comprehensive pact that the perception by the membership that such a document would have to be policed and enforced was simply not comprehended. It soon became evident, at each executive committee meeting as well as the infrequently held general meetings, that the report from the Grievance chair would be the longest and/or highlight of the assembly.

As the fledgling public sector union movement after the 1960s gathered momentum and matured, especially at the state level, so did the substantive and procedural aspects of the grievance process at the local level. It is perhaps best at this juncture to inform the reader, risking an insult to his/her intelligence, about the inner workings of what this author believes is a general gross ignorance of the grievance process, its purpose, and its effects. For instance, in the early days of collective bargaining there was little conscious thought given to the wording of a clause in an Agreement save for its effect on either expanding or contracting either of the bargaining parties powers or obligations. The phenomenon which developed as the collective bargaining process became more sophisticated and complex, and which also came to influence actual negotiations in a primal fashion was the issue of the enforceability i.e. effectively grieving, of the language of the Agreement. Words such as "will," "must," "shall," "may," "should," "can," and "in general" took on monumental proportions as they manifested their presence as one of ultimate success or failure of one arbitration after another. It became and remains axiomatic that the language of the Agreement both in its written form as well as in the intent of the parties determines what powers and rights either party to the Agreement is capable of legitimately exercising.

It was of course, within this setting, i.e., the grievance process, that yours truly found his niche. The whole process of evaluating the alleged grievance to assess its merit, the research involved (the Agreement, Education Statutory Law, Commissioner's Regulations, the Board of Education Policy Manual, Teacher's Handbook) and the writing/preparation of the case, was a challenge. I reveled in it! To me it was a labor of love. Former friends' and colleagues stated that if you scratched beneath my surface you would find a closet lawyer. Although my personal thoughts and/or feelings about the legal profession as a whole are less than enthusiastic, I have always admired and been slightly in awe of those who know and apply the substance of law in an ethical manner.

My experience and application within the grievance process was not ordinary. What made it unique was that I prepared and argued all grievances through each level of the process inclusive of the arbitration stage. It was at the arbitration stage that my baptism of fire took place, for it was here that the Board of Education brought its so-called big guns into the fray. It might be instructive to the reader at this juncture to divulge the various stages of the grievance process which is more or less standard in the vast majority of teacher contracts. The reader who has knowledge of private sector contracts may be somewhat amused by the bureaucratic and prolonged character of a teacher's Agreement grievance procedure.

In general, the process takes the following format. First, there is an informal stage consisting of either verbal and/or written statement regarding the complaint or charge being made by the grievant. This level usually involves the complainant/grievant, his/her supervisor (usually the principal of the building), and a union representative. In the Agreement, this informal stage is usually preceded by a philosophical statement wherein both parties agree to make every effort to come to some satisfaction of the differences which separates them. The wording obviously varies in all contracts but the intent and admonition is consistent— grievances are bad and show a failure of one or both parties to communicate and carry out its obligations under the Agreement! This failure is akin to a mortal sin and the consequent necessity for the use of the grievance procedure is an admission of their professional inadequacy to live up to their obligations without third party intervention. It might be informative for the reader to know that teacher contracts are unique from most other public and private labor agreements, in that they quite often include declarations of commitment sprinkled liberally throughout the document in order to establish some sort of philosophic legitimacy on the part of both parties.

It is important to note that at the first three stages/levels of the grievance procedure the hearing officer is either an administrator or member of the Board of Education. In the case of the former, it is more likely than not his act or omission thereof was the cause of the alleged grievance. Therefore, it would truly strain the imagination to conclude that the aggrieved teacher could expect an unbiased and impartial consideration of the complaint let alone a positive response to the redress sought. The time and effort spent by the teachers' union and Board of Education moving ever so slowly toward a decision could have been better spent if both sides compromised their positions somewhat and reached a decision that both parties could live with.

In the two and a half decades this author served as Grievance Chairperson, you could count on one hand the number of decisions which were rendered favorably to teachers at the first three stages of the process. As a result of the bureaucratic tangle inherent in the procedure, it was more the rule than the exception that the processing and arguing of a case typically consumed approximately four to six months. This schedule, of course, assumes that all four steps, including arbitration, were exhausted. It is, therefore, fairly obvious that it was to the employing Board of Education's advantage and interest to selectively observe the Agreement knowing full well that any attempt to circumvent it placed the clock on their side. It is generally acknowledged within the grievance/arbitration community that winning half of all grievances argued is not a bad percentage. This arguably being the case, it may be in an employer's interest to violate, misinterpret, and/or inequitably apply the terms of the Agreement whenever necessary. Caution, however, is necessary. As mentioned previously, the type of conditional wording such as "may" or "will" and "shall" or "should" indicate's how far and how often the District is prepared to share the cost of an arbitrator and set potentially dangerous precedents.

This brings us to the individual into whose hands both teachers and school districts are delivered—the arbitrator. He (we never experienced a she) was a lawyer, a member of the American Arbitration Association (AAA) and trained primarily in the art of determining the meritoriousness or lack thereof on the part of the employers' or, on extremely rare occasions, an employee's wrong doing. The arbitrator is controlled in arriving at any decision, by a single consideration—the written language and intent of the Agreement. He cannot object to, change, add, or detract from the contractual language. He must be convinced by the grieving party that the meaning and intent of the written word was either purposefully or by contingency violated, misinterpreted, or inequitably applied by the respondent school district. Testimony and evidence at the hearing is rendered under quasi-judicial conditions. Witnesses testify under oath and may be cross-examined as well as sequestered.[2]

The cost of arbitration over the years was relatively stable, averaging somewhere in the neighborhood of one to three thousand dollars per hearing. Included in the price was the hearing itself, travel expenses, room and board (no motels or McDonald's), consideration, writing of the decision, and postage.

Arbitrators are an interesting breed. They occupy a position of near-absolute power to decide the fate and future of individuals and an entire school district's plan of operation.

The selection of the arbitrator may be one of the most critical decisions that a union or school district can make. A key determination to be made is whether to have a different individual for each proposed hearing (a per diem arbitrator) or a permanent arbitrator mutually chosen by both parties to be the hearing officer for the Agreement's duration. Experience has shown that the decision to install a single, permanent arbitrator works to the benefit of both unions and school districts in the long run. A permanent arbitrator who serves for a period of three to five years gets to know the players fairly well. He gets to know the dynamics of the District's labor-management relations and some of the fundamental problems which plague both parties. The major drawback to having a permanent arbitrator is that he/she may be either a closet pro-management or pro-labor personality and end up benefiting one party over the other.

As a final post-script on the arbitration process I believe that it is grossly misunderstood by the general lay public because the primary contact with it is through the media and generally within the context of a national or an industry-wide crisis. I place much of the blame for the public's negative and often confused attitude toward arbitration on professional sports. More often that not what is perceived by the general public to be an open and shut case of misconduct or criminal behavior on the part of some multi-millionaire athlete turns out to be a partial or complete exoneration of the alleged charges. The newspaper account of the incident prominently mentions the ruling of the arbitrator relative to the litigation route. Interestingly enough the arbitrator often becomes the object for vilification by the ignorant, under-informed public.

It is not the author's intent to arouse the reader's sympathy for arbitrators as individuals or as a class. The intent is to shed some light on the arbitration process in both the public and private sector. In the private sector, as distinguished from the public sector, a unique set of circumstances has emerged since multi-millionaire athletes felt the necessity to unionize themselves. What has resulted in the offing is a labor-relations nightmare and a lawyer's dream. Whether knowingly or otherwise the stage was set for a two-tiered system of collective bargaining, contract interpretations and enforcement. Each athlete in each sport, with few exceptions, is protected by two collective bargaining agreements—his/her personal contract and the league contract between the franchise owners and the players collectively. With each professional athlete having an agent, a rather intricate dichotomy was created between the collective interests of all the athletes and each individual athlete's self-interest.

As for the collective bargaining between the league's owners and all the players, it becomes an interesting point of law, both in terms of labor law and contract law, as to which of the contracts takes precedence in a given situation involving managerial and player rights. For instance, if a clause in a league's collective bargaining agreement bans the payment of salaries during a player'' walk-out or strike, what control does it exercise if all or some of the individual players' contracts call for guaranteed annual salaries? How does the law deal with this dilemma, especially when two different arbitrators decide the issues and their decisions are in opposition?

No such confusion exists in the public sector, since personal agreements/contracts are generally illegal or non-binding. This condition exists because the union is the exclusive bargaining agent for all unit employees and boiler-plate clauses in almost every Agreement bar any individual agreements or arrangements which may be contrary to or inconsistent with the collective bargaining pact. It is obvious, there-fore, that an arbitrator's decision in the public sector, all other things equal, will create a more powerful precedent affecting the employment terms and conditions of all unit members than in the professional athlete arena where a dual contrac-tual relationship exists.

It is this author's firm conviction that the internal labor-management relationship which was established in the early days was irrevocably lost when both the school boards and teachers' union decided to go professional. By this it is meant that those individuals sitting at the negotiating table and act-ing as chief spokespersons were trained professionals whose interests in a local school district's labor-management rela-tions was limited primarily to time and remuneration for their services. In all candor, as one of my less favored superintend-ents used to say, the fault for the development of this change in negotiating methodology must be placed at the doorsteps of the Boards of Education and the Superintendents of Schools. I believe that research would support me in my asser-tion that the prime instigation for the switch to paid profes-sionals came from the offices of Superintendents of Schools.

The Taylor Law's enactment was obviously not greeted with any great enthusiasm by any public sector employer. School districts were especially reactionary to such legislation since it significantly reordered the nature of administrator's and teacher's relationships. Pre-Taylor Law relationships had been almost totally vertical with the Superintendent of Schools and building principals occupying an authority posi-tion somewhere between the Vatican and Billy Graham. The historical precedent of sitting down together at a table as equals and collectively determining the terms and conditions under which employees and employers would pursue their respective missions was, to say the least, traumatic. Many Superintendents, unfortunately, found the experience demeaning and unworthy of their exalted positions. It would not take long for them to convince their Boards of Education that a Superintendent's mission was too sacrosanct to be burdened by such time-consuming and unprofessional activities as collective bargaining.

The Superintendent (Chief School Officer) based his/her argument on the rationale that the teachers' union was using professionals in collective bargaining and, therefore, so should the District. The fact of the matter, however, was not quite as the Superintendents portrayed the situation. Indeed, the local unions were using professionals, but in the vast majority of cases not at the bargaining table. The statewide teachers' union, the New York State United Teachers (NYSUT), and the National Education Association (NEA) were being utilized as resource and training centers with an appropriately staffed legal division. The teachers for the most part represented themselves at the bargaining table.

This author believes that when the Chief School Officers (CSO) abdicated their seats at the bargaining table, they lost two vital opportunities in which to exercise their legitimate role as CSO. First, by remaining at the table during the negotiating process, they would have learned first-hand about any and all problems existing in the district and what made it tick. Secondly, Superintendents could have exercised their leadership role as both educators and a mediator in reaching a final conclusion to negotiations. One of the two superintendents who rates an A+ in my book of administrators did exactly that in our District's very first contract talks in 1967-68. This man could say no when it was necessary, but he also knew when to say yes. His capacity to be forthright, honest, and forceful created a mutual respect on our part, the union's team, resulting not surprisingly in the softening of our position on a variety of issues. He was the primary reason why we brought in the first contract in our District's history in a timely fashion. I remember in our newsletter to the association membership (we weren't quite ready to use the word union yet) that our negotiating team commented on the fact that the Superintendent of Schools had played a key role not only in fashioning the Agreement's terms and conditions of employment but had used his influence as an educator to have the Board of Education recognize teachers as professionals and co-equals in the educative process. He left us two years later. It never happened again!

Who were the professionals who became the surrogates for the Board and the Superintendent? Nine out of ten times they were lawyers. A number of law firms who had been general counsel for a school district quickly appreciated the advent of a new source of revenue—labor relations. Those firms with vision beefed up their staffs with labor relations people and assigned current staff to crash courses on Education Law and the Taylor Law. As a negotiator and grievance chairperson, this author's experience with the legal profession ran the gamut from professional expertise and demonstrated integrity to indifference and questionable ability. Whatever the case, it was the legal profession, as usual, that benefited handsomely from the new law, its application, and adjudication. As a non-member of the legal fraternity, I posed a bit of a problem to my counterparts who had obtained the much-revered Juris Doctor (J.D.) degree. A number of them looked upon me with contempt as if to say, "How can this common social studies teacher even assume to present himself as a legal representative and, worse of all, an equal to me, who has graduated from law school, passed the bar exam, and is a practicing attorney?"

At the outset I will admit that I was somewhat in awe of those who held the Juris Doctor degree. Experience, however, soon revealed to me that the degree meant little if the necessary case research and preparation were absent. It was in this substantive aspect of the law that I found myself to be the equal if not at times superior to my legal adversaries. It was unfortunately in the procedural arena that I experienced the most embarrassing and ill-prepared moments. At one time, the Board of Education had lost four grievances in a row at the arbitration stage and were anxious to reverse the situation. They fired their professional representative and brought in a high-powered local labor lawyer who coincidentally also represented other local public unions. The first case that the union brought to arbitration in which the new his man was involved appeared to vindicate their decision. The union's case was not the strongest in terms of merit but nevertheless was of sufficient import that it required an arbitrator's input. Due primarily to procedural maneuvering involving testimony and evidence, yours truly ended up not only arguing the case but serving as chief witness for the union's case! The Board's lawyer, again the Napoleonic figure, strutted and circled around the room like a shark homing in on its victim. After five hours of agonizing cross-examination, hyperbole, and posturing, the case came to a merciful conclusion. The arbitrator, our permanently installed one of ten year's tenure and himself a lawyer, admonished the gloating barrister with the following commentary which I now paraphrase, "Sir, although you are being paid to successfully argue the Board of Education's position, your persistent haranguing and badgering of the witness (yours truly), may cause an ill will that transcends this evening's proceedings. You will leave tonight. These people (union and school district) must remain and live together." Now deceased, that arbitrator brings back fond memories.

The local union's statewide professionals, NYSUT, were not of the same stripe as the Board's hit men. A number of them were former teachers and in one way or another were interested in and connected to the teaching profession. Where the district's representatives were there for the sole reason of monetary compensation, the NYSUT representatives were generally more emotionally involved and they really did care what happened to the classroom teacher. However, as professionals, they also took the path of least resistance and allowed local unions to settle for contractual language and compensation that in the long run was not always to the local membership's advantage. This was due in part to understaffing accompanied by an increasing workload demand. If the local membership felt it could live with an Agreement's employment conditions, then NYSUT said okay, and moved on to the next school district.

Overall, NYSUT, affiliated with the AFL-CIO, has over the years done an effective job of representing teachers, lobbying for legislative security, promoting teacher welfare, and providing an exceptional legal department for the defense of teachers' legal rights and privileges. It is one of if not the most powerful state teachers' unions in the nation. In concert with its AFT affiliate in New York City, it brings tremendous clout to the legislative forum where both Democrats and Republicans alike seek out funding and are sensitive to its agenda. The NEA represents the remainder of the teaching corps in New York with a membership of approximately 25,000, out of a total of over 350,000 teachers.

Although the degree of antagonism exhibited in the private sector between the AFL and CIO prior to their merger in 1955, such has not been the case between the AFT and NEA although a philosophical gap still exists and persists. The failure during the summer of 1998 of the NEA to adopt the articles endorsing the merger of the two national teacher unions is testimony to the on-going historical antipathy that both teacher organizations have had and continue to have towards each other. It is this author's visceral reaction that the NEA, the older and larger of the two, regards itself as the true and perhaps purer representative of teachers and educators, untainted by the defiling touch of the private sector labor movement personified by the AFL and CIO. When and if the NEA finally purges itself of this preordained position and both organizations are merged, look out Washington![3]

Moving towards a more intimate view of local teacher unions and their internal power dynamics allows the author to share some experiences and insights into their functioning. As in all organizations which engage in the representation of an active and growing constituency, teacher unions at the local level have also experienced a metamorphosis of sorts. This transition has affected teachers at all levels—state, national, and especially local. Many teachers have come to believe that the teacher union movement is somehow unique in the annals of the labor movement. Nothing could be farther from the truth. Its uniqueness, if any, lies in its tardiness on the scene. Myths, however, are difficult to erase and certain individuals in positions of leadership within the educational labor community have carefully cultivated them.

Perhaps chief amongst these inventions was the idea that teacher labor agreements/contracts benefit not only teachers but the student body and the entire community. Smaller class size demands and inclusions within the Agreement were cited as district benefits to the children and their parents. Class size is an especially attractive argument to today's baby boomer parents who seek to maximize individual attention to their offspring within the school environment. The fact that small class size meant fewer papers to correct and fewer discipline problems to deal with was underplayed, as well as the parallel ingredient that smaller class size meant more teachers, and more teachers meant higher budgetary requirements. The reader must not misunderstand the author. The teachers were intelligently pursuing a time honored American labor-management axiom—the fewer the hours, the greater the pay. As in the private labor sector, this did not necessarily mean that the worker was shirking one's duty to perform the required tasks efficiently but that the effort and/or time necessary to do the job could be reduced. Greater productivity would be a natural outcome, argued organized labor, and society as a whole would be the beneficiary with more and better products. Other than monetary remuneration, class size and class load weigh most heavily upon the classroom teacher as factors which most affect professional status and the capacity to perform one's duties. American students, especially in the urban setting, bring much baggage to school each day. A teacher with ten students has ten non-academic problems to deal with. Nowhere else in the civilized world and especially in the industrialized nations of the world does this type of educational environment exist.

Other myths most critical to comprehending the psyche of the teacher labor movement, rested upon the bedrock article of faith that teachers, among all other professions, were somehow more special, more dedicated, more reliable, and more critical to the national interest and society's well-being. We believed that by some cruel distortion of fate these

unique qualities had been taken for granted and undervalued by American society in general and that newly obtained
collective bargaining rights of the 1960s would be the means
to correct this misappropriation of society's values. Testimony
to this belief is the consistent use of rationale as well as philosophical jargon in all teacher contracts, especially as a
means of explaining why class size is thirty or what the purpose
of a sabbatical is, to name a few. Boards of Education and
Superintendents of Schools must also share the credit for inclusion of such language. While the union's motives tended to
be a bit more sincere, the School Boards and their administrative spin doctors had a more sinister motivation, namely to
emasculate any contractual language they had been forced
to agree to which had diminished their managerial prerogatives. A classic example would be that which pertains to class
size, a critical article for both sides, historically. Try this class size
provision for openers—"Minimal Central School administrative
officials and the ...Board of Education have always been
cognizant of the need for classes to be of reasonable size,
generally 23-28, where this meets practical criteria.
Therefore...in order...for those students who are in school to
have the greatest advantages for learning and the most
effective conditions...in reference to teacher-pupil ratios,
these administrators and Board members agree with the
Association that it will be the School District's goal to have no
more than 28 students in any regular elementary and academic classes. Further, it is agreed that class size in excess of
these numbers...should generally be avoided except for a
limited period of time. When classes do exceed these numbers consideration shall be given to making provision for some
special assistance."

Teachers, administrators, Board members, arbitrators,

lawyers, and union representatives will immediately recognize the quicksand which underlies this actual clause from a current teachers' Agreement. However, for those readers not intimately acquainted with the language and subtleties of teacher union Agreements the described words hopefully illustrate to the layperson the extraordinary lengths to which both teachers' unions and school districts will rationalize and hypothesize a contract provision until it is virtually meaningless. Much of the blame, if any is to be made, lies with the district's administrators and/or Board of Education, who seek to weasel out of any kind of language which forces them to be accountable. As districts hired lawyers to represent them at the bargaining table, the language of contracts became more laden with evasive and emasculated clauses as exemplified in the preceding excerpt. Unions tried the same ploy but much less successfully since they actually wanted an Agreement, and needed to have certain items such as class size included. Half a log was better than none.

Another field of battle and one which has created a vast storehouse of somewhat imaginative case law, if not fascinating dialogue, is in the job action arena. Since by law most, if not all states make it illegal for public employees to strike. One of organized labor's most intimidating weapons has been denied to them. For teachers especially, given their innate feelings of mission and importance to society, this statutory ban has been a major impediment. What does that leave teachers with as an effective instrument of action to assert effective pressure on a reluctant Board of Education? In fact, very little of real substance.

What teacher unions create is an illusion of power and control. The illusion is created primarily in the press and on television. This method is the high road and generally includes interviews, advertisements, and attendance at Board meetings. It is there that the union's president will make an impassioned speech highlighting the teachers' increased frustration with the lack of a new Agreement and the devastating effect this has had on morale. If the Board is smart it will thank the union's president and its members and go on to its regular agenda. This gentle and orderly treatment frustrates the union's membership even more. If, however, some Board members who are less astute decide to get into a debate or discussion on the issues at the bargaining table then they play into the hands of the union. Union leaders will be quick to point out to an eager press that it is the Board of Education who has precipitated the current crisis and is to blame for the stalemate, as evidenced by their hostile attitude.

The low road is one which is as repugnant to the teachers themselves as it is to the Board of Education and the community at large—informational picketing and work-to-contract. In the former, teachers who really don't consider themselves to be labor must carry signs and parade in front of schools or other prominent local gathering places and walk in circles. This action's purpose is to demonstrate solidarity (a favorite union slogan) to the public and publicize that all is not well in the school system. From a purely personal point of view picketing was like an Irish wake where seeing colleagues you haven't talked with in a while and exchanging pleasantries of sorts become as important as the deceased, in this case the Agreement. There were always the hard-liners who reminded people not to smile at each other and to look appropriately grim. This demand never ceased to amuse yours truly.

For some members picketing was a welcome outlet for their pent-up hostilities as well as artistic tendencies. For this type of union member sign making became the ultimate challenge in outwitting the Board of Education. A silent contest of sorts was set into motion as members attempted to out-slogan each other and come up with the most attention getting slogan that would capture the entire essence of the bargaining crisis in a few pithy words. It was of interest to note that certain moribund members of the teachers' union were reenergized by the prospect of a public display of unhappiness.

The other low road tactic, work-to-contract, generated the greatest degree of antagonism not only between the union and the Board of Education, but within the ranks of the union members itself. For the uninitiated reader the term is used to describe the action taken by the instructional staff to confine their activities and duties to the minimum prescribed by the contract. While an explanation of the term appears to be straightforward, nothing of the kind is in fact the case. Although a teacher's terms of employment are governed by a multiplicity of both written and non-written proscriptions, it is the Public Employment Relations Board (PERB) which in most instances is the final arbiter in determining what constitutes a legal or illegal job action.

With the teachers' union adoption of a formal work-to-contract resolution, the technical legality of such action immediately comes under the purview of PERB. What constitutes a legal or illegal job action has provided PERB staff and lawyers for both unions and school districts with a fertile field for interpretative judgment. Since the entire premise of the work-to-contract hypothesis rests upon the assumption that by limiting teacher duties and responsibilities to the confines of the written Agreement both District authorities and parents would experience a reduction in the services previously rendered. This reduction effect would result in a diminution of teacher contact and effort due in large measure, if not entirely, on what teachers have always maintained has unrecognized and generally uncompensated voluntary and extra-legal work.

Activities such as back-to-school nights; staying after school to assist students; volunteering to oversee student plays, clubs, and field trips; and displaying student work on bulletin boards have all been declared by PERB and the courts as activities "...within the scope of their teachers responsibilities which must be performed after the close of the regular school session." The courts have further ruled that, "An agreement by conduct does not differ from an express Agreement...Thus, it is clear that an agreement...can arise from the conduct or acts of parties as well as from their words." In conclusion, the courts have sealed the fate of work-to-contracts by stating unequivocally, "...that...the day in which the concept was held that the teaching duty was limited to classroom instruction has long since passed and teachers are well aware of the fact that there are some activities [which] have by custom and usage, been regarded by both the administration and by the union members as part of their teaching duties and professional responsibilities!" It is therefore apparent that the so-called weapons at the disposal of teacher unions are few in terms of effectiveness and the application of real leverage. What is left to the teacher unions is basically rhetoric and symbolic unity of purpose such as entering and leaving school buildings en masse at contracted times.

In matter of fact most of the time-honored weapons available to labor in the private sector have been eliminated for use in the public sector. Henceforth, public sector labor-management disputes have been reduced in effect to appeals from both sides to the general public for support for their respective positions. Protracted labor-management disputes tend to become ugly with each side portraying itself as the real victim or savior depending upon the issue at hand. In the case of school, concern for the students and the delivery of services to them becomes the paramount issue. It is obvious that with the Taylor Law's statutory and prevailing case law prohibition, the teachers' unions are hard-pressed to utilize any service reductions that effect student activities. As with nurses and their patients, so too are teachers extremely reluctant to indulge in any work action that would jeopardize their students' health and achievement.

Although it may be said that a school is a family of strangers, it is still family nevertheless. The term in loco parentis has more in its meaning to a teacher than its legal definition. As a matter of fact the student issue, especially in protracted labor-management disputes, is one of the primary causes of internal union dissension. It is due in great part to the degree that a specific job action will affect the student body's access to teacher services. The smaller the school district the more amplified the dilemma becomes when the choice of job action and its consequences puts teachers against one another in what should be a common union cause. In the case of a strike, and they do happen despite the two for one penalty in the Taylor Law, the animosity between strikers and non-strikers tends to endure over the years. Former friends now exchange icy stares as they meet in the morning at their mailboxes. Faculty meetings will tend to divide along adversarial lines based upon the personal decision to strike or not. The wound never heals completely as former colleagues are permanently transformed and alienated from each other.

What follows are vignettes and/or remembrances from the union movement as I knew it.

• *In the early days of collective bargaining, the Board of Education's chief negotiator uttered such a pithy remonstrance as, "Is the squirt worth the squeeze?" and "If it's fiscally sound, it's educationally sound," or "Gosh, be reasonable, fellas!"*

• *The union President whose primary raison d'être was to have women run the union and turn the men into followers and/or eunuchs.*

• *The hot-blooded ethnic whose blood boiled once very three years during negotiations but was curiously silent and somewhat unavailable during the interim.*

• *The young negotiator/grievance chairperson who sat under the American flag in the faculty room and held audiences, à la the Godfather.*

• *The tough, former nun whose primary mission in life was to cause a rush of cold manure to the heart of every administrator by both her presence and mere mention of her name.*

• *The Superintendent of Schools, whose code name was the Zipper or Zero, who admonished the student body one year in a written Papal Bull to stop throwing objects out of school bus windows when an irate parent informed him that a student had thrown a moon at her from a school bus.*

• *The handful of teachers who each year refused to join the union but gratuitously accepted all of the benefits included in the Agreement.*

• *The supermediator whose skill and perception of the bargaining process brought us in three successive years in a row after marathon bargaining sessions.*

• *The same mediator who promised to hold yours truly in contempt when during stalled talks I threatened to walk out and go home to see my favorite John Wayne movie.*

• *The old kindergarten teacher who was part of one of our early bargaining teams remaining wide awake and alert while many of the rest of us youngsters fought to stay awake during a marathon, all-night bargaining session. She was a great lady.*

• *The subconscious contest among the sign makers for the most pithy and original posters that their eager fellow colleagues/picketers could display.*

• *The gatherings on the picket lines where after being instructed to project a sullen and angry demeanor the teachers projected a professional look punctuated by smiles, hellos, and lets-have-coffee-afterwards greetings!*

• *The meeting at which the membership voted to implement its first job action—informal picketing—in order to protest stalled collective bargaining. The decision to participate in a public display of dissatisfaction was a difficult one for many teachers. Some left the meeting while others looked down at the floor as the activists (yours truly among them) vehemently exhorted the membership to make a show of unity.*

• *The day the local union voted to take away the active member status from retirees and deny them their voting privilege. It was a sad day for unionism, especially when one union faction seeks to deny another's franchise.*

• *The number of teachers I defended during grievances and arbitration proceedings who I knew I would have probably fired, but argued for and in many cases won remuneration and/or reinstatement. Many never thanked me or even said hello afterwards.*

• *The two union members who lied under oath while giving testimony in an arbitration proceeding to whom I never spoke again. One of them was openly proud of his deception. The other one didn't know the difference.*

• *The permanent arbitrator our district and the union shared for ten years.*

Even when we lost a decision, I admired and understood his logic and rationale. It was sad to see him lose his acumen and witness his mental deterioration in his later years.

• *The perennial witness as our permanent arbitrator termed one of our teacher chairpersons who it seemed had pertinent testimony to offer in almost every case, no matter what the grievance issue.*

• *The Board of Education, disgusted with their failure to win four arbitrations in a row, firing their representative and hiring then area's top labor-management lawyer. It was difficult for them to accept the fact that a social studies teacher was beating them at the grievance table.*

• *The look of amazement and utter dismay on the part of the administrators at the bargaining table when yours truly brought in almost 20 teachers as consultants for our initial bargaining session. Much protest was made by the administration about the fish bowl setting, as they stated it.*

• *The look of dismay which never failed to appear when certain Superintendents and principals observed me entering their buildings/offices.*

Amen.

Notes

1.New York State School Boards Association, School Law, 27th ed., (Albany: New York States Board Association, Inc.,. 1998), 224.

2.Ibid., 245-246.

3.Thomas H. Johnson, The Oxford Companion to American History, (New York: Oxford University Press, 1966), 210.

Chapter Eight

Potpourri

8

Potpourri

We live in a growth society economically speaking, where marketing is the key to survival. No one and nothing is left untouched. That includes education. Plato and Socrates would have failed miserably in such an environment and perhaps even Christ. A socio-economic environment does not encourage scholarship and the search for truth, but instead idolizes the Henry Fords, John D. Rockefellers, J.P. Morgans, and Bill Gates. And that's all right as far as it goes. But would the reader categorize any as true givers? They were takers who became givers only after they had secured all that they wanted and then achieved a salvation of sorts through widely publicized philanthropic acts.

No so for the teacher-scholar class. The educator's private sector competitors, through cost/benefit tactics and the exercise of the owner-entrepreneur prerogative, exert a degree of product quality control unheard of in the halls of academe. The public school has little if any control over the raw material—its students—that it receives and unlike its private school counterpart cannot be selective in who it admits or dismisses.

Let us assume for the sake of discussion that the teacher and/or educational institution provides a service—education—and that the consumer is the tax-paying public. This places the student in the category of being the product. Allowing for these proposed socio-economic labels we can begin to discern the broad outlines of what Marx would have portrayed as an inherent contradiction in terms.

The general consumer public has historically transferred the economic axiom "you get what you pay for" from the marketplace to the classroom. The greater the cost of the product, the greater was the expectation of its quality and utility. A guarantee, although limited to some extent, gave the consumer a modicum of protection. If the product proved faulty and incapable of functioning it would be returned for a refund or replacement. This process however, is inapplicable to the educational experience.

Present-day critics of the public schools would have us believe that any school, with certain qualifications, should be controlled solely by the fundamental laws of economics. As an example of such reasoning they apply a simple input/output system. Under this device inputs such as resources, capital, and labor are applied to the production process. Output, or productivity, is measured in terms of the ratio of input to output. The effectiveness and/or efficiency of the operation would be evaluated on the basis of minimizing the cost and amounts of the inputs and maximizing total output. The differential between total cost, i.e., input factors, and total revenue, i.e., output multiplied by price, would equal a plus or minus profit. Although this equation oversimplifies classic input/output analysis, it does reflect on the underlying philosophy of the most vocal critics of the public schools. They use privatization in the guise of consumer choice to educate all of our youth.

At the risk of sounding like a defrocked Marxist, economic determination is presently the tail wagging the dog of edu-cation. An increasing number of so-called educational reformists measure the success or failure of the educational institution primarily, if not solely, on a scale of economic effec-tiveness/efficiency. Again, facing the hazard of oversimplifi-cation, we can agree that price times quantity (or output) equals total revenue.

Substituting educational terminology into the equation-begins to shed some light on the rationale for the negative assessment being made by critics of public schooling. The price times the product, i.e., a functionally competent and capable student-graduate, equals a total revenue to the nation, i.e., world-class achievement, that does not justify the current expenditure for public school education.

The proposed solution to this inverse relationship between costs and benefits is to implement the economic law of sub-stitutes. Simply put, the law of substitutes states that as the price (P) of product Y increases, the quantity (Q) demand for its substitute, product X, will increase. Therefore, cry the school's Greek chorus of critics, the application of pure eco-nomic reasoning mandates a change in the productive process. This option, however, is unavailable according to logic because public education is a monopoly of the state. In other words, the tax-paying public has no effective substitute to opt for with their tax dollars unless they wish to enroll their children in a non-public institution at additional cost.

It is at this point that the condemnation of the schools takes on a decidedly free market or free choice flavor in order to justify the much touted voucher system's necessity. Herein tax dollars are dispensed to the education consumer, or tax-paying parent, who then enters the education free market to select the school that best meets the educational goals and/or aspirations for one's children. Choice/voucher proponents say this will result in all schools competing for tax dollars and instructional personnel, with the concomitant effect being the upgrading of accountability and the quality of the educational product. There are other residual effects, mostly economic, but the primary consideration, say its advocates, is the competition in a free market.

Let us pause for some reflection on the issues of choice and competition in a free market. The hallmarks of a purely competitive or free market are an unlimited number of competitors/firms, price competition, an undifferentiated product, and ample ease of entry and exit out of the market. These are the characteristics of a free market which the champions of school choice, if they are to remain credible, must advocate and apply toward the operation and management of the nation's education system.

Consider the following scenario based on the fundamentals of the classic free market structure. First, in accordance with the criteria of an unlimited number of firms, i.e., schools, we can perceive a proliferation of schools and philosophies catering to the programs and agendas of sundry interest groups. They will appeal to the innate prejudices of consumers espousing gender, class, and racially motivated doctrinaire ideologies. What the standards will be in these schools that will have any degree of national consistency, not to mention consensus, is anyone's guess.

At this time in our nation's history when a national curriculum cries out for implementation, we are experiencing instead a swing in the opposite direction. These proponents of choice in education, not the politicians who see votes, belong too often to the same faction that advocates states' rights and the downsizing of the federal government's role in people's lives. The proponent's major objective is to return to a confederation of states wherein the Tenth Amendment to the Constitution preempts de facto Articles I-III of the Constitution while expanding the powers of the states. This objective is closely associated, and works in concert, with school choice promoters who vision an unlimited number of schools being loosely controlled at the state/local levels as it originally was in the eighteenth century. This is a recipe for domestic educational disaster.

In a study of world class schools, undertaken by Donald M. Chalker and Richard M. Haynes of Western Carolina University, a comparison of selected national education systems revealed that countries such as France, Great Britain, Japan, Israel, Korea, New Zealand and Taiwan have all moved towards national standardization of curriculum and goals. The United States, in contrast, already deviates from this norm and has by far the most fragmented system of curriculum and goal development of any of the so-called world class schools. In an era when the diversity of the American population has reached an apogee and ethnocentric and/or racial consciousness has become the raison d'être for increasing numbers of Americans, the proliferation and constant institutionalization of a variety of curricula and standards bodes ill for a United States.[1]

This Balkanization of our educational institutions will be further exacerbated by the second tenet of a free choice market structure—price competition. It is upon this bedrock of capitalism that the pro-choice advocates of competition among the schools rest much of their case. As any first-year economics freshman will be able to confirm, prices are determined in a competitive market by the laws of supply and demand. Promoters of choice, such as voucher systems,

would have us believe that parents receiving a direct payment from the government to matriculate their children in a
school of their choice will cause the currency of education to
appreciate. Their thinking goes along the following lines: an
increase in the demand for entrance into top caliber schools
will bring an inflow of money into same. Those schools not in
demand will be forced to take measure to improve their programs so that they will be able to compete with existing
schools of choice.

This argument is appealing on its surface. However, closer
scrutiny reveals a critical flaw. It dismisses certain basic tenets
of economics. The law of supply, for instance, is conveniently
ignored or minimized. The sources of funding and the quantity
of funds available under the present systems of financing are
limited and are becoming more so. When referring to supply,
we are talking about the supply of schools not of money.
Remember, we are referring to consumers who are demanding a product—the functionally competent and capable student—in conjunction with the producer/supplier of that product, the schools. Assuming a free choice scenario, we will in all
probability witness an increase in the actual number of schools
as home-schoolers, active and/or retired educators, religious,
ethnic, and corporate entities organize themselves into educational institutions. Due to the proliferation both qualitatively
and quantitatively within the fifty states as well as the lack of
effective national leadership and purpose, this school growth
projection is not an unrealistic one in the short run.

In the long run, the dynamics of the market will reduce the
number of schools if not school districts as the supply curve
shifts upward and to the left and becomes more inelastic or
less responsive. The original proliferation of educational institutions will shrink and a reduction in both school districts and the

number of schools within individual districts will probably result. The reason is obvious. The financial sources available for public funding of education are relatively fixed. In economic jargon such a condition is referred to as a budget restraint. The voucher funding supplied to parents in order to exercise choice will shift funds to specific schools that will benefit at the cost of those institutions that will experience the loss of both students and financial resources. A parallel example can be observed in the commodities market exchange (COMEX) where, unlike the securities stock market, for every winner there must be a loser.

"The rich will get richer and the poor will get poorer," states the old adage. Poor urban/rural school systems currently experiencing shrinking tax bases with few prospects for additional funding will suffer further erosion in their physical, technological, and curricular delivery systems. Perhaps the most devastating outcome of the free choice scenario will be the widening of the socio-economic schism that already separates the disenchanted minorities from the rest of society. The volatile and holocaust threatening issues of racism, multicultural ethnocentrism, and economic disparity will be greatly exacerbated. E Pluribus Unum may well be alluded to by future generations as a non sequitor. Instead of the enhancement of our educational institutions, we shall undergo a metamorphosis which will magnify our group prejudices and further divide an already factional society and nation currently on a collision course with itself.

We now focus our attention on the third characteristic of a free choice market, namely, product similarity contrasted to differentiation. Do the proponents of choice want to produce a student body that is identical in its characteristics, achievement level, and preparation? In a purely elastic demand market where all products are generally equal or near perfect substitutes for each other, there would be no provision for or necessity to differentiate between the products produced by a variety of independent firms. Competing firms manufacture commodities that resemble each other, but no firm can exist if they do not differentiate their goods from those of their competitors. The customer must be able to perceive something different and attractive in a product in order to want to consider it for initial and continued consumption.

It therefore becomes axiomatic that in a highly competitive environment a firm faced with a large number of competitors will be forced to resort to non-price competition. Resourceful and innovative rivals will advertise the various attributes of their product line in order to woo customers from each other. They will link utility or satisfaction with price or cost in order to subordinate the competition. Advertising and promotion of the attributes of a product line in the short-run assist in creating competition. In the long run, increased expenditures/outlays needed to maintain a separate and popular identity critical to continued customer satisfaction may in fact become anti-competitive.

Can the reader discern, after lifting the corporate veil, how the concept of product differentiation and identification in a competitive market environment is applicable to the educational experience? The present demand for choice in the selection of educational institutions will universally put into motion market forces which are governed by the fundamental dynamics and consequences of economic law. The increased necessity to distinguish graduates and institutions from one each other will result in the dilution if not elimination of a national education platform when it is needed the most.

The marketing that will be required of public schools will

parallel that of the private schools that promote their institutions by proclaiming the congenital high quality of their graduates while developing in them an appreciation for strong moral and ethical values. Can the public schools, given the myriad of mandated regulatory and statutory sanctions under which they must function, compete effectively with their private counterparts who are relatively free of such authority? The answer is an obvious "NO!" Therefore, if real market conditions are to prevail in the education industry, then all the competitors must be governed by the same economic and regulatory restraints.

The proponents of free choice or privatization in education would reduce or eliminate what they perceive to be the monopolistic restraints of an overpowered educational bureaucracy. How would they reform the nation's schools so that a competitive environment could prevail? If they are truly sincere about applying free market forces to the process of choice in education, then their model is the prevailing one of corporate behavior. Such behavior in the marketplace would be governed by profit maximization, cost reduction through downsizing of labor inputs, and replacement of labor through increased technology and elimination of inefficient units or their reabsorption into larger cost-effective entities. We have only to observe the results since the 1980s of these economic realities, especially in the manufacturing sector of the economy to weigh its eduction application.

A critical question now emerges. Is it economically feasible to have the structure of competition with many competing units but not be exposed to the above-mentioned behaviors of competition? The proponents of choice would have you believe so. Such an assertion flies in the face of economic reason and logic.

With their interpretation/application of economic pre-
cepts to the education process, the free choice advocates
conclude the following.

*1. That a purely competitive market can exist in which some of the compet-
ing units are restricted in their conduct while others are relatively unrestricted,
such as private schools.*

*2. That consistent downsizing of the labor force—teachers—in order to
reduce costs, and the concomitant replacement of them with technology will
improve the delivery of educational competence and achievement.*

*3. That the downsizing of the labor force will attract more qualified individ-
uals into the education profession.*

*4. That labor-management relations will improve because potential union
members will decline as the aging teacher population is replaced by technology.
Union cooperation will increase in direct proportion to its loss of membership and
job security will replace wages/benefits as the top priority in the collective bargaining process.*

*5. Eradication or severe curtailment of tenure laws and certification require-
ments will give local school authorities the flexibility to hire/fire a professional
instructional staff in accordance with local ideological and economic desires.*

*6. Repeal or diminution of statutory authority or effectiveness in labor-man-
agement relations will allow local school authorities the option of entering into the
collective bargaining process or, at worst, severely limit the number of issues/sub-
jects identified as mandatory topics for negotiations. By narrowing the scope of the
collective bargaining process, budgetary economies of scale may be realized.*

The preceding conclusions would find a welcome haven
in the board rooms of corporate America for it is there that
they have had their embryonic origins. The free
market/choice advocates have as their inspiration and role-
models that entrepreneurial class that gave and continues to
give our society merger mania, treatment of labor as a cost-

sheet statistic and not as a resource to be developed, the elimination if not severe curtailment—as Adam Smith sagely observed—of competition, and the replacement of the labor force with technology.

Their entrance into the education market has already taken place with questionable results at best. Educational Alternatives Incorporated (EAI), the Edison company, and Advantage Schools, Inc. are notably firms that have spear-headed the charge for the privatization and for-profit opera-tion of the schools. Two large urban districts, Hartford and Baltimore, were the primary clients of the Minneapolis-based EAI. Both school systems have severed their original contrac-tual relationship with EAI. The experiment lasted for fourteen months in Hartford and for approximately three and a half years in Baltimore.[2]

The reasons and causes for the apparent failure or lack of success are varied depending on which side or faction is heard from. What all the rhetoric can basically be reduced to is caveat emptor and caveat venditor, which means buyer beware and seller beware. The assumptions and expectations of both buyer—school district—and vendor—EAI—were obvi-ously not reciprocated. The pivotal element in the relationship between the private sector (EAI) and the public sector (schools) was their different perceptions of the extent of the economics issues involved and the educational outcomes that were to be realized. Both parties recognized that the common problem was controlling the spiraling costs of running the schools. For the educational establishment privatization was looked upon as a desperate attempt to reduce the cost of educating children while simultaneously increasing the level of their achievement. Those officials in authority or majority who made the decision to invite the private sector to manage its classrooms did so in the philosophical belief that the private sector was somehow better equipped organizationally to more effectively conduct the business of education than a public sector counterpart. It was and is unfortunately an assumption shared by too many American citizens. What was ignored was the fact that the product to be manufactured was the development of a human mind, not a widget.

As the late and honored Ernest Boyer, former president of the Carnegie Foundation for the Advancement of Teaching, commented," It's almost impossible to say 'no' to choice in the abstract." In a nation like ours whose roots are historically planted in the soil of freedom of choice and anti-authoritarianism, it is in Boyer's words, "almost un-American." Hence, those critics of the public schools who wrap their displeasure for the educational system in the mantle of disenfranchisement are acting out a charade. They are not interested in reforming the system, but instead are determined to destroy it by guaranteeing its failure. Its failure will be assured by the expedient of imitating corporate organizational management principles in concert with cost-benefit economies of scale. As already commented upon, we cannot have the structure of corporate organization without also experiencing the behavioral consequences of accountability to stock holders and increased adversarial confrontation between labor and management.

Akio Morita, the mastermind behind Sony, aptly critiqued corporate America's Achilles' heel in its struggle to compete effectively within the international community. An obsession with short-term profits in order to satisfy stockholders, poor labor-management relations, and the lack of patience to await the results of long-term capital investment. An educational system, likewise, fragmented into fifty autonomous corporate entities, each professing the goals of high standards and student achievement within a cost-effective and profit motivated vehicle, is the recipe for a national catastrophe.

This writer in his experience is all too familiar with the failures, ineptitudes, and shortcomings of our public schools. They have been addressed within the confines of this book. It is the general philosophy of the so-called reform movement of the free choice advocates that has been dealt with so far. It is their contention that the schools have failed and, therefore, must be reorganized and reinvented. This writer obviously does not share their extremist view. What he does share is their desire for a change of direction and the need for communal involvement with schools and schooling. Much of the machinery for change is already in place. All that needs to be done is to fully utilize the present system. Where reform is truly needed is in the sources and methods of funding our educational system. The lack of equity in providing the resources necessary to place all children on the same starting line is a national scandal. This is the fundamental issue of the school choice debate—funding and equity.

No one likes to be taxed. Our nation was founded on the principle of "No taxation without representation." It is the latter part of that familiar cry that is at the heart of the free choice faction's displeasure. They believe that choice is the simple panacea for the funding/equity problem. It will cleanse the system of its infirmities and restore vigor and potency to its performance. A similar theory prevailed in the medical sciences during the eighteenth century when worthy physicians bled their patients to remove bad humors. Most historians are of the opinion that such a practice was the primary cause of our first President's demise, which reaffirms this writer's opinion that the proponents of school choice and/or privatization want to bleed the present public school system and replace it with a market-oriented, consumer driven substitute.

This author is not against the exercise of choice in principle. It is a concept and modem whose time has come. What this author objects to is the hidden agendas and self-serving motivations of its messianic agents. I am reminded of the Chinese Mandarin scholar who after being exposed to the Western idea of Christianity observed that there was little to criticize about its philosophical tenets. What aroused concern in him was its practitioners, the Christians. And so it is with educational choice. As Peter W. Cookson, Jr. notes in his expansive book "School Choice: The Struggle for the Soul of American Education," a wide range exists in the types and application of choice. Behind each model, however, at the risk of sounding paranoid, lies a scheme which has as its ultimate objective the satisfaction of redressing some grievance(s) held against society at large, a political authority, or the so-called educational establishment. As Cookson observes in his book, school choice can trace much of its origins to the white flight from the public schools following Brown v. Board of Education of Topeka (1954).[3]

Those at the extreme end of the spectrum would seek vouchers from the government to educate communities and/or households which espouse isolationist and cultist doctrines inspired by antisocial ideology. The moderates would use the voucher system to allow parental choice both within and outside of the school system but only for public schools. Those advocates of greater market choice would use public funding for choice of any school system, both public and private, sectarian and non-sectarian.

Perhaps the most intriguing entry of the choice plans is the charter school model. This concept combines much of the voucher/choice/privatization philosophy into a single entity existing within a school district, but basically independent of it. The state authority and/or local school authorities would be requested to issue charters to groups of teachers, parents, or community members who would be responsible for their operation. Such schools would receive the same amount of public tax money per student and be given a waiver for state education rules and regulations, local school board policies, and labor-management contracts. The quid pro quo for receiving such dispensation and retaining the charter is an agreement to be held accountable for achieving certain specified academic goals. Although the current number of such schools is slightly less than 2,000, the emotional appeal made by its supporters in the name of entrepreneurial competition is attracting considerable attention.[4]

It is of interest to note the somewhat ironic if not hypocritical stance that the so-called reformers/chartists take in order to assure their success. They continue to be in the vanguard of the most critical factions of the public schools with their accusations of monopolistic and non-competitive practices and bureaucracies. Yet, in order for their charter school operations to take hold and survive, they require that special consideration in the form of waivers covering statutory requisites, instructional staff certification, labor contracts, tenure provisions, and curriculum guidelines to be granted.

In international economics jargon such a request is referred to as the infant industries argument for protection vis-à-vis a tariff/quota placement against foreign competition. The question is when does the infant grow up? The charter school proponents, who so vehemently espouse a competitive environment governed by choice, would initiate their endeavor within the same environment and/or conditions that they accuse the public schools of presently existing in.[5]

The charter school innovators have already run into the bane of all school systems and types, namely, financing. The have discovered that starting a school is more than spouting idealistic notions and gathering children to seek truth in the universe. The original amateur hour does not work in the halls of academe.

Specialists, trained and credentialed, in all phases of educational pedagogy are necessary. You would not want to arrive in an operating room for removal of a tumor only to overhear the anesthetist and surgeon discussing plans to initiate and/or complete their studies in order to carry out your operation successfully. Why then would parents wish to expose their children to, in many cases, a start-up entrepreneurial operation which cannot guarantee any results? The answer, based on this author's experience with parents and the public, is cause for great concern because it is predicated upon personal and self-serving agendas.

As previously stated, present day parents seek to obtain to the greatest degree possible an individualized program tailor-made for their child's unique needs and abilities. The IEP is a plan, formulated by the professional staff in conjunction with parental consultation/approval, aimed at providing the instructional environment needed to assist a child with psychological or physiological restrictions to achieve to his/her fullest capacity. This is what all parents want today—an IEP for their child.

Therefore, behind the current rhetoric of choice, competition, and accountability lies the fundamental cause of disenchantment with the public schools—my kid is not getting the education he/she needs in order to develop his/her unique talents/personality to the optimum. With this revelation in full view it becomes more comprehensible why and how the public schools have been set up to fail and satisfy the self-fulfilling prophesies of each self-interest group. Herein lies the basis for future politicization and associated legislation which will dominate the educational agenda in the future. The public sensing polls will increasingly quantify a candidate's position vis-à-vis his/her rival in terms of their stance on educational choice. It has already occurred in the primaries that led up to the presidential election, wherein all declared candidates for that coveted office came out in favor of some form of parental choice. Instead of a dialogue based upon the coined adage E Pluribus Unum, we will instead have to remint our coins to read E Pluribus Pluribus.

The public must be educated, perhaps by the schools themselves, that school choice and its assorted allies cannot resolve the profound issues currently being placed at the doorstep of the schoolhouse. The problems of socio-economic justice and equity, unless truthfully confronted, will irrevocably injure this nation and especially its children. The market advocates, who refer to children as educational products, have either forgotten or are ignorant of the Greek root of the word education, which literally means to lead or draw out. Again, we should look to the East as a mentor, where the experience of learning is what is prized most, not just the product.

As Cookson has aptly stated, "Schools may not transform society, but schools can transform the lives of children…" The only question is will they be allowed to? Schools at any level were never created to transfigure a society into some utopian paradise. As asserted previously in this chapter, the official and popular perception of the schools was to preserve and promote the political, economic, and social status quo. Much of that changed in post-World War II America. Instead of maintaining the status quo, the educational institution was to become the agent for change. It was not only to prepare for change, but to plan, devise, and implement socio-economic change that would alter/correct society's failures. What other institution can the reader identify that was ever expected to perform a comparable assignment?[6]

What then is to be done? This author does not pretend to assume that mantle of a Delphic oracle. But if a series of issues is addressed in a cooperative and non-confrontational manner, they would result in reforms/solutions which might prove satisfactory to a majority of Americans. Before embarking upon this odyssey, I must offer one pre-condition or qualification to the ensuing discourse, namely, that we assume that all schools move toward and/or adjust their educational goals/objectives to meet world class standards.

A definition of world class is obviously in order. As a guide both in defining the terms and in listing its component features, I will again use the 1994 study previously mentioned by Donald M. Chalker and Richard M. Haynes. The objective of their research was to provide a uniform set of world class education standards and to compare those criteria with the United States education system. The authors selected nine nations plus the United States as possessing world class education systems. They were Canada, France, Federal Republic of Germany (West), Great Britain, New Zealand, Republic of China (Taiwan), Israel, Japan, and the Republic of Korea (South).[7]

Ten categories with thirty-five norms were used to define world class standard, which represented the numerical mean of the ten countries. The ten categories measured were: educational expenditure (percent of gross domestic product

(GDP) spent on all education, per capita GDP, and public per pupil expenditure), instructional or time on task (average days, hours, minutes of instruction), class size (primary/secondary school pupil-teacher ratio), teachers (years of higher education, classroom atmosphere), student date (percent of students reaching final grade offered in school, percent of thirteen-year-olds who watch five or more hours of television daily, percent of thirteen-year-olds who spend four or more hours on math/science homework per week), curriculum (organization of primary/secondary curriculum), standardized test evaluation(who prepares, purpose, results available to public), governance of the schools (national, state, local control, percent of students in private versus public schools), and home and community (national literacy rate, student suicide rates, rate of divorce per 1,000 persons, parental involvement, number of TV sets/daily newspapers per 1,000 persons).[8]

Each of the selected categories fundamentally influenced the effectiveness with which student learning and achievement were affected. Americans must therefore comprehend what it is that they hope to achieve as they enter into the debate to determine the future model(s) of our schools. To this writer it obviously should be a world class school system. Interestingly enough, my fellow Americans like to talk about competing effectively with other countries on a world class level but all too frequently avoid defining the beast. I suspect that to most Americans world class means being numero uno. I seriously question, however, whether the majority of my fellow citizens truly are willing to make the personal, economic, and political sacrifice necessary to achieve such lofty status. We talk a good game and in the past believed that if enough financial resources were thrown at the academic community they would eventually cure society's socio-economic problems and turn out a superior product, i.e., the graduate. As alluded to in previous chapters it did not happen.

Partially using Chalker and Haynes' categorical delineations in conjunction with my own suggested qualifications, the following recommendations are humbly proposed as a possible course of action:

A. The federal government must increase its financial and educational leadership role. Maintaining the status quo is unacceptable. Of all the world class nations, the United States has the most fragmented and decentralized educational system. It is a convenience that has seen its day and must be replaced by a national curriculum and national testing standard guided by the national goals we want to strive for. When the population of our country was 3.5 million at the end of the 18th century or 31 million during Lincoln's presidency or 100 million at the turn of the 20th century, we were able to afford the luxury of numerous autonomous state-systems overseeing a vast multitude of quasi-autonomous localities. Today, we are the third largest nation in the world with approximately 285 million people. The luxury ceased to exist in the post-war era as defeated former enemies as well as allies reorganized and reconstructed their economies, in some cases their governments, and in all cases their educational systems in order to meet or make the competition in the ensuing world order. During this period the Unites States was distinguished by its failure to recognize the need for reform and, therefore, failed to make any real substantive changes in its educational house.[9]

B. The financing of education at all levels will remain problematic if not outright disastrous in the coming century unless Americans and their political representatives make a sincere bipartisan resolve to fund education on the basis of equity and need. Recognition of the reality that urban and non-urban wants and needs require different responses will go a long way towards achieving equity within a world class standard. Urban school systems in varying degrees must be recognized for what they are—war zones within a supposed education environment. During wartime, dramatic and extraordinary measures are needed. If ultimate victory is to provide equity with world class criterion for all of its student body K-12, then our urban educational systems must be in a quasi-military sense be considered the most vulnerable parts of our fortifications. The bulk of the nation's financial resources earmarked for education must be significantly increased and concentrated in inner-city schools. A generation of African-American and Hispanic youngsters must not be discarded and written off as casualties of a war that was lost because we would not make the sacrifices and take the action necessary to succeed.

It is this writer's conviction that the following financing/ funding proposals be adopted at both the federal and state levels in order to provide the resources necessary to achieve world class standards in the education of our youth.

1. That property taxes be gradually and systematically reduced over a period of time but not completely eliminated. This action would shift the incidence of taxation and result in a less regressive imposition on homeowners and hopefully a concomitant reduction in the antipathy towards schools.

2. That in lieu of or in addition to the three dollar contribution to presidential campaigns currently available on tax forms, it be earmarked for the express purpose of being used to invigorate and restore our urban schools.

3. That all taxpayers receiving refunds be given the option of contributing five dollars to both national and state governments respectively for the purpose of technological upgrading and expansion of school facilities.

4. That for those taxpayers filing long-form tax returns a provision be included that allows additional dependency deduction in the calculation of those individuals or married couple's adjusted income tax when donations to a school of their choice is equal to or exceeds $2,500.

5. That the source of funding be shared equally between federal and state authorities. The overwhelming majority of world class school nations reveals a pronounced percentage—60 to 90 percent—of funding originating at the central government level.

6. That all public and private schools who qualify upon application receive an annual per pupil stipend of $7,000 per annum to be applied toward each student's education, K-12. This sum would be shared equally by the federal and state governments.

7. That a national lottery/drawing be held twice annually in which the proceeds realized after prize awards and management fees are deducted be earmarked solely for educational use by the nation's schools. This voluntary form of taxation would assist in the financing of the previous recommendation (number 6). The proceeds would be allotted to the states on a formulated need basis.

The aforementioned recommendations are a relatively painless, if the term may be used, attempt to increase the variety of sources available to educational funding and ease the burden of taxation incidence so that the tax albatross effect is less severe.

As in all attempts to reform an existing system whether it be the principle topic under discussion in this book or in engineering, medicine, or the law, a linkage factor must be addressed and dealt with. In education the link between funding sources, methods formulae of distribution, and qualification and identification of recipients, must be viewed and treated in a universal manner. Being the recipient of public funding carries with it the burden of qualification and continuous monitoring. For instance, the present British reform system that was implemented in 1988 and modified in 1993 is a partial-oversight model. It should be considered as mandatory for all public and private schools in order to qualify for public funds.

First, a national curriculum should be pursued and adopted with dispatch. A consortium of educational, business, and political leaders in concert with parental and teacher representatives must dialogue, establish, and write a national curriculum. A top down process should develop macro-objectives/goals which will allow for a conciseness of sorts and yet remain broad enough to provide for local adaptation. The major obstacle to the adoption of a national curriculum, its substantive issues aside, is the issue of fifty educationally sovereign states. Due to the historical and constitutional vacuum created by a lack of federal/national provision, the educational prerogative became the responsibility of state/local authorities who under the tenth amendment came to not only exercise the sovereign will but became the repository of sovereignty in the education of the people.

Given the mosaic that makes up the religious fabric of American society, the much-touted inclusion of ethical/moral instruction can be easily immersed into a diatribe of conflicting doctrinal values. This should not be allowed to happen. A consortium of responsible leaders at both national and state levels, representing religious, agnostic, atheist, educational, political, and historical interest groups should convene and develop broad objectives along with subordinate specific values that are reflective of our nation's historical mission and the legitimate hopes and desires of a patchwork quilt population. It won't be easy. Even the Japanese with their chronicled experience of homogeneity continue to debate the current form as well as the necessity for ethical/moral training. Was Hobbes correct when he observed that life would be "...short, nasty, and brutish..." if mankind was left with too few constraints on personal freedom and its unfettered exercise?

The concept of the comprehensive high school should be carefully reevaluated. The European/Japanese models which selectively track students and place them in an educational environment wherein their substantive needs and skills are more effectively met and developed might be emulated. Vocational or specialty schools are not to become dumping grounds or warehouses for mandatory age non-scholars but challenging environments demanding the utmost in effort.

A working relationship, not just a public relations one, between high schools, junior/community colleges, and vocational/specialty schools could result, if approached properly, into an effective tool to kindle a flame into the minds/hearts of so many of our disenchanted and uninspired youth. Such schools would offer a challenging and demanding curriculum in which its participants upon graduation would possess sufficient skills to compete effectively for jobs in both the manufacturing and technical service sectors of the economy.

The standards of achievement in the scholastic high school and/or the comprehensive high school should be set at levels at least equal to those required in France, Germany, and Japan. In all cases, whether vocational or scholastic, no student should be allowed to graduate without passing an exit or school leaving comprehensive exam. Students of mandatory age, i.e., sixteen, who fail such an exam should be retained to age eighteen on either a full-time or part-time basis, until they have mastered those skills required by the national standards of the schools.

The aim/objective especially of the scholastic or comprehensive high school of the twenty-first century should be to graduate or produce citizens whose exposure to and achievement in a broad spectrum of subject matter and related skills would allow them to enter into any sector of the economy with the entry-level skills needed to perform any assigned tasks efficiently and competently. Specialization in the scholastic/comprehensive high school would be counterproductive since the skill level, motivation, and aptitude of these students are much broader-based than in the vocational student population. For many of these students a premature specialization could possibly eliminate or subsume latent talents and abilities which in the future would better serve the individual as well as work to the benefit of society. The scholastic high school graduate should possess a variety of technical and human skills which will allow him/her to exercise choice effectively for further educational and/or entry into the economy as a productive agent.

In relationship to a proposed national curriculum, it is only logical that some sort of national testing/evaluation be introduced. The timing of such an assessment of student achievement should occur twice, with the initial evaluation coming at some point between the fifth and seventh grade, followed by a second appraisal at age sixteen. Overtesting should be avoided as the British found out. World class countries limit testing to two or three levels. Their example should be followed. The group/consortium that constructed the national curriculum should also construct the national testing guidelines. This should guarantee a considerable degree of consistency in terms of reliability and validity between the two. The utilization of the test results should be aimed at assessing current student achievement in light of critical curriculum assessment and as a procedural device to direct student placement for future vocational/academic advancement.[10]

As Chalker and Haynes indicate, the future goal of American education should be the development of a national examination which would be administered to students completing the academic/college preparatory program. This writer would also advise the development of a national vocational examination which would be reflective of those elements and skills which a student would require for immediate entry into the manufacturing and/or service sector of the economy. The successful students on these national exams would qualify for entrance into a college/university or in the case of the vocational track, for effective and immediate entry into the productive community.[11]

Notes

1. *Chalker and Haynes, 120.*

2. *Mark Walsh, "Education, Inc.,: The New Business of Schooling," Education Week, Vol. XIX, No. 13, (1999): 14-15.*

3. *Peter W. Cookson, School Choice: The Struggle for the Soul of American Education, (New Haven: Yale University Press, 1994), 121-122.*

4. *Walsh, 14.*

5. *Peter B. Kenen, International Economics, (Englewood Cliffs: Prentice Hall, 1964), 29.*

6. *Cookson, 130.*

7. *Chalker and Haynes, 2-3.*

8. *Ibid, 4-7.*

9 *Ibid, 21-215.4*

10 *Ibid, 243-244.*

11 *.Ibid, 246.*

Chapter Nine

Since Retirement?

9

Since Retirement?

In 1993, after thirty-three years before the mast, I took my leave of public school teaching and proceeded to make application to a number of two and four-year colleges. In both ignorance and somewhat egotistical perception of my own self-importance I eagerly awaited for the flood of invitations from the world of higher education. The resulting response was illuminating to say the least. It was with more than a little regret that I became aware of a pattern which seemed to be developing among the letters of rejection which came in the mail. It was my age. I had never at age 55 considered myself as old. The word experienced was how I defined my chronological status. It was worse than my brief traumatization years before when I received my initial AARP eligibility notification.

Although I was obviously aware of the emphasis on the youth culture in our society I was psychologically unprepared for its negative impact on my own occupational ambitions. There it was, and I felt helpless to deal with it. The reader may question my self-evaluation and conclusion about the age issue, but in my mind there was no doubt. The aforementioned pattern of rejection was experienced in both academic and non-academic job openings. In most instances, I was either overqualified and/or highly qualified for the vacant position. I was not even given the benefit of an interview by any of the academic institutions despite my apparent qualifications. It was only in the private sector that I experienced the interview process. But, alas, the result was the same—rejection.

The frustration and anger which overwhelmed me was partially aimed at those people who had failed to see anything of substance other than my age. It was also aimed at my own self-delusion for not being conscious of a fact of life that others had to face. My retirement, which had coincided with my attainment of a doctoral degree from New York University, was not to be the end of my educational career but was to be Chapter Two instead. I was not prepared mentally or physically to accept the possibility that there would only be one chapter. I had been the eye of the storm for my local union for twenty-five years. Freshman had quaked in their shoes as they entered my bastion of medieval scholarship. Seniors expected a college-level experience and had received it. My image as a teacher, disciplinarian, and union leader were unchallenged. However, it was now all over and the ignominy of being a non-participant and suddenly invisible terrified me.

It was during the first two years of retirement that I truly realized how much I missed the action of the classroom. It had been my raison d'être but I had not fully appreciated the depth of its hold on me. With no offers from academia, I embarked on a three-year sojourn of fillers as they say in the newspaper business. I tried substituting, at my wife's behest, both in private and public schools. In the former I had to establish in seven hours the reputation as teacher and disciplinarian that it had taken me a generation to achieve. In one public school I became known as the 'psycho' substitute because of my penchant for orderliness and expectations of academic excellence/performance. That brief interlude lasted all of two days and reinforced my suspcions that all per diem substitute teachers have one foot in heaven and the other on a banana-peel. The private school experience was antiseptic in the sense that it represented the opposite spectrum of indulgence. There, every teacher was: 'Sir' or 'Madam'. No discipline problems only Lake Woebegone enfants with 'all above average' credentials. It was pleasant but one could never really tell whether you were doing a helluva job or were merely being tolerated as a means to mommy's and daddy's 'ends'.

Between 1993-95, I entered the world of the 'legal beagles' and became an educational consultant with a now defunct law firm. It was to say the least an educational experience. A former public school student of mine who had obtained his juris doctor degree cajoled me into joining the firm. My duties were varied, ranging in breadth from research on the re-cycling of discarded tires to acting as mentor/advocate for high school age students in need of legal and psychological guidance. I handled all of the cases regarding student mentoring that came into the office. The experience offered me an insider's view of what I had only guessed at when it came to parent-child relations over the years. My appreciation of what parenting a high-school age adolescent involves expanded ten-fold as a result of this assignment.

My case-load involved three families. Each of the three families was dysfunctional to a significant degree. In the first family, the mother was on her third husband and the daughter needless to say had had three 'fathers'. The school-related problem in this case invloved attendence at school ot the lack thereof. My research on the law, i.e., case law and

Commissioner's Regulations along with an analysis of the local school district's attendance policy gave us sufficient 'ammunition' to strike a deal in which the somewhat reluctant 'scholar' would be allowed to make-up both time and study which had been lost. A combination of teacher turnover (three different instructors); poor and inconsistent record-keeping; and a poorly constructed attendance policy, were the key players in obtaining a second chance for our client.

As a side note, I couldn't help but sympathize with the parents whose economic status must have been somewhat desperate in their effort to come up with my fee, i.e., $75.00 per hour and the lawyers fee, i.e., $100.00 per hour. Although they could not afford us they took out a loan in order to pay us. I had mixed feelings in this endeavor. I *had* earned my fee, but for some reason I recalled a character in the Merchant of Venice who had required 'a pound of flesh' for his fee.

My second case, which incidentally I was working on simultaneously with my attendance policy case, invloved a young man who was also an attendance problem and came from a divorce-separated environment. He was a bright young man who unfortunately lacked both direction and motivation (a common adolescent malady). It was my assignment to meet with him on a regular basis as well as with his teachers in order to work-out some kind of a program to improve his attendance and concentrate more effort on his studies. It was a difficult, if not unique experience for me to sit at a long table with my 'fellow-colleagues' and perform a function that only a short time ago I might have held in disdain as just another means of getting a student 'off the hook'. It was not a comfortable position and I felt somewhat awkward. My efforts met with mixed success. The young man's lack of purpose and commitment in close association with his parent's incapacity to deal with him or each other eventually led to a break-down in the firm's professional relationship with him. I don't know what happened to him.

Once again the financial issue raised its Godzilla-like head as the father, who I felt was the most concerned parent experienced difficulty in meeting our fee schedule. But I was learning fast. Unlike my experience in the labor wars of teacher unionism where I was emotionally as well as professionally involved in my responsibilities, my experience in the land of jurisprudence and barristers had taught me the art of uninvolved involvement. My Japanese studies background had given me a phrase to define my role: kirisute gomen, 'the right to execute and walk away.' I had represented my client, ably I believed, but in an unattached manner which somehow bothered me.

The word client has a disembodying quality to it which renders its object to a somewhat dehumanized condition. My emotional involvement in the professional and often personal lives of the teachers I had represented over the years left me unprepared to face the 'detached' world of the law. Friends had encouraged me over the years to study law and become a lawyer, but I always knew that the classroom was my vocation. The law, i.e., public labor law, was my avocation. It has and still holds an unrelenting fascination for me. However, I never saw myself as a lawyer. For over thirty years I had dealt with them as a resource; as a representative and as an opponent and even as a friend. No matter their personal and professional character, they all shared one common trait: detachment. I believe the saying within the legal profession states in effect, that: 'an individual has a fool for a client when he/she represents themselves.' Further, it is my comprehesion that the aforementioned axiom is an example of a lawyer's greatest fear: involvement/attachment with a client.

In 1996, still somewhat frustrated and anxious about my seeming inability to be 'restored' to my element of the classroom, I drew up two courses of study for the local Teacher's Center. Thanks to the cooperation and encouragement of two exceptional women at the Center, I was able to teach once again in my two areas of specialization: Asian Studies and Educational Law. The excitement of being back in the classroom where my knowledge and background could be utilized to assist my fellow colleagues was overwhelming. I was too embarrassed to admit even to myself just how much I had missed it! I was subconsciously concerned, however, whether my penchant for teaching was making of me a one-dimensional personality. But then upon careful consideration I said, "What the hell? At my age (59), who needed multiple personalities?"

It was in 1997 that my first so-called 'break' occurred. Russell Sage College in Troy, New York, contacted me about my interest in supervising student teachers. I leapt at the opportunity probably alarming the college's caller, when I said "Yes!" without hesitation. This assignment proved to be one of the most rewarding of my career. The obvious reasons for my desire to become involved with the new generation of teachers was clear. Primary among these reasons was the desire to share almost four decades of active classroom experience with young men and women who believed that they wanted to be teachers. My motives were also somewhat selfish in that I wanted to observe first-hand and evaluate what was going on out there in the local school districts. My particular assignment involved observing and mentoring both undergraduate and graduate student teachers who were placed in semi-rural, suburban, and urban public and private school systems.

An individual could easily write a book or even a novel based upon what one can observe in one day in an individual school. Each school has a personality and flavor all its own. To the general lay person who observes from the outside looking in, such a phenomenon is basically unknown. Therefore, a school district can develop a personality or, better yet, an attitude towards its educational mission. Each school takes on an identity of its own tempered by the district's overall attitude and/or philosophy.

It was this factor that I immediately sensed whenever I entered a building in which a cadet or student teacher had been placed. Certain qualities and characteristics readily asserted themselves and caused early judgments to be made by an observer. Some characteristics may appear minor in scope but when viewed in the aggregate create a portrait of sorts. Among the items which emerge are locked front doors (this may indicate something), condition of floors/hallways (papers/garbage), noise level when students are in classes, how visitors are greeted in main office when checking in, presence and frequency of hall monitors, teacher/faculty room (location/condition), professional staff appearance/dress, frequency of classroom interruption by public address system and/or other persons, attitude towards strangers (assistance/ignore), student attitudes toward each other and staff members, and general condition of the building.

There are other factors. The preceding are those that hit you the quickest and hardest. It was these factors that affected my perception at the outset and weighed significantly in the final evaluation of the young men and women under my stewardship. The extent to which these externals affected the overall performance of a cadet were carefully weighed on the scales of both objective and subjective judgment.

The single greatest evaluative variable was the student population within the regular classroom. The second variable in importance was the status and reputation of the cooperating teacher. It was a bit of a revelation, although not a surprise, to be witness to some extremely well-organized and capable teachers. Granted, not all of the cooperating teachers were paragons of pedagogical accomplishment. But the overwhelming majority of them made me proud to share the title of teacher with them.

The primary variable in the cadet teacher's experience, the student, reinforced almost every conviction and sentiment that I had harbored over the past four decades. As I have often stated, American students are the most demanding in the entire world. They expect your maximum output and effort. In return they more often than not give you their minimum. As for their attitude towards student teachers, all other things being equal, it can resemble at times a feeding frenzy among sharks. They smell blood and move in for the kill. It doesn't happen in every class, but it does happen too often to too many young, aspiring teachers. The American adolescent can be a master of disaster within the confines of the school environment. Their techniques of disruption and task avoidance have been skillfully honed. It can be as subtle as in the case of an entire class apparently bored and engaged in a quasi-ignoring of the young cadet's presence. In less subtle circumstances it can degenerate into boisterous outbursts aimed at either the student teacher and/or at fellow students. A full day of quelling sporadic rebellions, listening to foul language, and experiencing an inherent disrespect for the educational process must at times be sufficient motivation for these young men and women to consider seriously another line of work.

The preceding scenario is one of the prime causes of the lack of substitute teachers throughout the nation and especially at the secondary level. Who would want to put up with this nonsense and humiliation for fifty to sixty dollars a day? Only a masochist! Teaching has always been a "shallange" as Clouseau would say. It is, however, the nature of the challenge which has made the classroom a battleground. A combination of reluctant, if not unruly, scholars, increased teacher standards, public skepticism and criticism of the schools, elevated student standards, higher expectations of pedagogical excellence, and a constant pursuit for respectability among the professions, are not exactly the type of inducements that attract and/or hold people to the profession.

There have been times when I have wanted to say to these neophytes, "Try something else and be appreciated." I never do because I realize how very critical they are to the future of this nation and the continued prosperity of its citizens. In an American society where an individual's worth is primarily measured by the level of wealth that he possesses and/or generates, the subjective value of education is somewhat ambiguous. On the one had we stress the significance of obtaining a good education which includes a college degree while simultaneously denigrating the purveyors of the means of achieving the same—the teaching profession. It is this strange symbiosis that the new additions to the ranks will somehow have to rationalize in order to seek their respective raison d'être. I wish them bon chance, they will need it!

In addition to my student teaching assignment, my services suddenly came into demand at a number of higher schools of learning. Through a happy circumstance of my personal availability and a series of leaves of absences/vacancies, a mini-cottage industry was created with yours truly being identified as a necessary commodity for the continued success of local collegiate programs of study. Utilizing my Asian studies background along with my experience in education law and the classroom I found myself employed by three institutions simultaneously. Time-wise, I was working almost as much as when I was a full-time public school teacher. Being in the right place at the right time is still axiomatic for success.

Each of the classes for which I was responsible gave me the opportunity to observe undergraduate and graduate students within a formal academic atmosphere. As expected, the graduate students, of whom all were obtaining master's degrees to teach, were by far the most intense and productive. They were committed and purposeful in their approach and attitude towards their studies. The undergraduates, in contrast, were generally somewhat indifferent both in their attitude and productivity. Their written efforts on both tests and research papers displayed a minimal to mediocre appreciation for the written word. I was disappointed but only mildly surprised to discover that the gap between high school and college in terms of quality was minimal. The same lack of direction and indifference to effort and a work ethic remained intact. Taking up space and time in a protected and relatively stressless environment seemed to be the modus operandi among them.

It is difficult for me to admit that perhaps the quasi-open admissions atmosphere that pervades the college admissions offices throughout the country may require some modification. I believe that a nationwide reevaluation of how and when an individual is admitted to higher education should be carefully examined. No one should be denied the opportunity to obtain an undergraduate degree. The qualifications and requirements for matriculation, however, must be raised so that the effort required to qualify for entrance is not so minimal that it debases the currency of a college education. This is a difficult proposition, but a necessary one, because it strikes at the very heart of the purpose and goals of higher education. I do not propose a return to the pre-World War II elitist concept of a university education à la the old boys preparatory schooling for a place in daddy's law firm or business. Instead, I believe the Japanese model holds a partial prototype for advancing the cause of qualifying students for a college level education.

In order to matriculate into the Japanese collegiate system, the high school graduate must pass a separate exam for each institution applied to. Special after-hours schools, called juku or cram schools, are attended in order to prepare for the rigorous entrance exams. Admission to higher education is an earned achievement, not a gratuitous award. In the United States it is almost impossible not to be able to find a college or university that will admit you into one of its programs. Then again, the Japanese do not have to struggle with the twin issues of affirmative action and minority quota requirements. An admissions entrance exam could have the effect of enhancing not only the quality of college enrollments but in motivated high school juniors and seniors to prepare more assiduously for a higher learning experience. Such an exam, in conjunction with the deified SAT score and other valid subjective criteria, would be a more logical standard for admission to a four-year college experience.

For those individuals either unwilling or incapable of

matriculating into a four or five-year college program, a one or two-year program should be made available in order to prepare people for a technology oriented career. Recent studies have revealed that despite the American economy's incredibly sustained growth in the nineties, the number of persons who remain on the welfare rolls remains relatively high. Furthermore, the labor seeking economic climate which currently pervades the nation demands skilled labor, i.e., technologically literate, to occupy those positions which the daily Dow Jones and NASDAQ markets are a reflection of. The community college organizational apparatus already in place should be promoted, financed, and marketed by a combination of government and private sector resources. A public relations campaign of sorts should be established on a nation-wide basis which would tout the quality and flexibility of such institutions. A coordinated national effort would serve to raise the status and effectiveness of a technology oriented community/junior college program while at the same time serving the needs of the economy.

In the private sector, which has expressed in recent years a growing discontent with the education establishment's perceived inability to produce efficient and well-trained graduates, I propose the following solution: start your own schools! Emulate the Japanese model by pressing for increased standards at the public school level and then educating specialists and/or generalists at the corporate level. Our high schools should graduate generalists who possess a variety of pragmatic skills in all of the major disciplines, such as math, science, etc. These young men and women would have three options in either continuing education; proceed on to either a two-year and/or four-year institution or seek employment with a company while simultaneously being educated within its corporate school. Federal and state governments could serve to motivate the foundation of such corporate schools by enacting legislation that engenders tax incentives of a friendly nature. Corporate America would be placed in the position of putting up or shutting up. Instead of seeking tax certiorari judgments in the courts as the primary means of lowering costs, the business establishment would be putting its organizational skills and resources to work in a more positive, if not effective, manner.

Whenever I meet someone who I once shared the same teaching space with, gather with former football teammate at college reunions, or just run into acquaintances at funerals the inevitable question is posed—what are you doing with your retirement time? My response usually evokes forced praise or talk of the weather. To many of my fellow retirees a gasp of subdued disbelief is expressed when I mention my current workload and four distinct education employers! In many respects I feel sorry for some of them. They devoted their entire lives to the education of our youth and were surrounded by children who depended upon them and looked to them for sustenance. Now they are mostly forgotten relics of another age. A few have their hobbies. A number ply their time between the sunnier climes of Florida or the Carolinas in the winter. The perennial cruises to the Caribbean in February and/or the visitations to the grandchildren where for a few fleeting hours/days they become the eye of the storm again are all too familiar patterns.

Although I have no vaunted research to support my claim, it is my belief that teachers who have left the classroom wars are similar in many respects to retired athletes who no longer experience the competitive wars. The rationale for this comparative analogy lies primarily on the commonality which both share in regards to their respective audiences. Both are the center of attraction and under the inspective scrutiny of their clients. Both of their audiences are fickle and can switch from unabashed adoration to scorn in an instant. Both of their audiences expect perfection and timeless commitment while reciprocating with sporadic bursts of total involvement balanced by degrees of indifference. Both are involved in a contest of wills, among varying opponents—teacher versus students, athlete versus athlete, teachers versus administrators, athlete versus coaches. Both bask in the warmth of their respective audiences' adulation and recognition of their efforts. Both innately feel that their mission/performance and sacrifices were not truly understood by the general public. Yet, in their retirement, they remember the good times more than the bad.

My tale now draws to its final curtain call. I have completed my goal of putting into words for posterity what being a teacher was all about for at least one lost soul. If one was to believe in the idea of predestination, then this author would be a primary source of evidence to support such a belief. For forty years the classroom has been the foundation of my existence. When I am in that element I am energized. Remove me from it or deny me access to it and the organism begins to wither. Unfortunately, but necessarily, my time as a seeker of truth and purveyor of knowledge grows dimmer with each passing autumn. Our nation is not a particularly good one in which to grow old. Age is feared, not venerated, with only the manufactured memories of past successes as a bulwark against oblivion. For a teacher, those successes are counted in the triumphs and achievements of one's students and the knowledge that in some small but significant way he/she was a causal agent of same.

Yes, without qualification I would do it all over again and pray that in my next incarnation I may be allowed to repeat the path that places me in the footsteps of the Buddha.

Selected Bibliography

Berliner, David C. and Bruce J. Biddle. *The Manufactured Crisis: Myths, Fraud and the Attack on America's Public Schools.* NEW YORK: ADDISON-WESLEY PUBLISHING COMPANY, INC., 1995.

Bunyan, John. *Pilgrim's Progress.* LONDON-NEW YORK: DENT, 1973.

Chalker, Donald M. and Richard M. Haynes. *World Class Schools: New Standards for Education.* LANCASTER: TECHNOMIC PUBLISHING CO., INC., 1994.

Cookson, Peter W. *School Choice: The Struggle for the Soul of America.* NEW HAVEN: YALE UNIVERSITY PRESS, 1994.

Dickens, Charles. *Great Expectations.* MILWAUKEE: RAINTREE, 1989.

Doyle, Arthur Conan. *A Treasury of Sherlock Holmes.* LONDON: HANOVER HOUSE, 1955.

Education Week. *"Quality Counts: A Report Card on the Condition of Public Education in the Fifty States." Ed. Ronald A. Wolk, Washington D.C.: Editorial Projects in Education, Inc., 1997.*

Encyclopedia of Education, *ed. Lee C. Deighton, vol. 9, New York: MacMillan Co. and the Free Press, 1971.*

Faulkner, William. *New Orleans Sketches.* Ed. Carvel Collins. New York: Random House, 1958.

Gandhi, Mohandas K. *Autobiography*: My Experiments with Truth. Boston: Beacon Press, 1966.

Hansot, E. and Tyack D. *Gender in American Public Schools: Thinking Institutionally.* Signs, 13(4), 1988.

Heilbroner, Robert. *The Worldly Philosophers.* New York: Simon and Schuster, Inc., 1986.

Hobbes, Thomas. *Leviathan.* London: Dutton, 1973

Kramer, Rita. *Ed School Follies:* The Miseducation of America's Teachers. New York, The Free Press, 1991.

Mitchell, Margaret. *Gone with the Wind.* New York: Avon, 1973.

National Commission on Excellence in Education. *A Nation at Risk: The Imperative for Educational Reform.* Washington, D.C.: U.S. Government Printing Office, 1983.

New York State School Boards Association. *School Law,* 27th ed. Albany: New York State School Boards Association Inc., 1998.

New York Times. *Education Life: "Is Experience the Best Teacher?"* Peter Applebome.

Schirokauer, Conrad. *A Brief History of Chinese and Japanese Civilizations,* 2ND ED. ORLANDO: HARCOURT, BRACE, JOVANOVICH COLLEGE PUBLISHERS, 1989.

Solzhenitzen, Alexandre. *The Gulag Archipelago.* NEW YORK: HARPER AND ROW, 1974.

Sowell, Thomas. *Inside American Education:* THE DECLINE, THE DECEPTION, THE DOGMAS. NEW YORK: THE FREE PRESS, 1993.

Spear, Percival. *India: A Modern History.* ANN ARBOR: THE UNIVERSITY OF MICHIGAN PRESS, 1961.

Su, Zhixin. "TEACHER EDUCATION REFORM IN THE UNITED STATES, 1890-1986." *In Occasional Paper, No. 3, College of Education.* SEATTLE: UNIVERSITY OF WASHINGTON PRESS, 1986.

U.S. Department of Education. *Schools and Staffing in the United States: A Statistical Profile,* 1990-91. WASHINGTON D.C., U.S. GOVERNMENT PRINTING OFFICE, 1993.